With Culture in Mind

D1707796

The Relational Perspectives Book Series (RPBS) publishes books that grow out of or contribute to the relational tradition in contemporary psychoanalysis. The term *relational psychoanalysis* was first used by Greenberg and Mitchell (1983) to bridge the traditions of interpersonal relations, as developed within interpersonal psychoanalysis and object relations, as developed within contemporary British theory. But, under the seminal work of the late Stephen Mitchell, the term relational psychoanalysis grew and began to accrue to itself many other influences and developments. Various tributaries—interpersonal psychoanalysis, object relations theory, self psychology, empirical infancy research, and elements of contemporary Freudian and Kleinian thought—flow into this tradition, which understands relational configurations between self and others, both real and fantasied, as the primary subject of psychoanalytic investigation.

We refer to the relational tradition, rather than to a relational school, to highlight that we are identifying a trend, a tendency within contemporary psychoanalysis, not a more formally organized or coherent school or system of beliefs. Our use of the term relational signifies a dimension of theory and practice that has become salient across the wide spectrum of contemporary psychoanalysis. Now under the editorial supervision of Lewis Aron and Adrienne Harris, the Relational Perspectives Book Series originated in 1990 under the editorial eye of the late Stephen A. Mitchell. Mitchell was the most prolific and influential of the originators of the relational tradition. He was committed to dialogue among psychoanalysts, and he abhorred the authoritarianism that dictated adherence to a rigid set of beliefs or technical restrictions. He championed open discussion and comparative and integrative approaches, and he promoted new voices across the generations.

Included in the Relational Perspectives Book Series are authors and works that come from within the relational tradition, that extend and develop the tradition, and that critique relational approaches or compare and contrast it with alternative points of view. The series includes our most distinguished senior psychoanalysts along with younger contributors who bring fresh vision.

RELATIONAL PERSPECTIVES BOOK SERIES

LEWIS ARON & ADRIENNE HARRIS
Series Editors

RELATIONAL PERSPECTIVES BOOK SERIES

LEWIS ARON & ADRIENNE HARRIS
Series Editors

RELATIONAL PERSPECTIVES BOOK SERIES

LEWIS ARON & ADRIENNE HARRIS
Series Editors

With Culture in Mind

Psychoanalytic Stories

Edited by **Muriel Dimen**

Routledge
Taylor & Francis Group
New York   London

Chapters 1–6, comprising Part I, "The Social Third," originally appeared in *Studies in Gender and Sexuality, 12*(1), 2011, pp. 1–37. Reprinted with permission.

Routledge
Taylor & Francis Group
270 Madison Avenue
New York, NY 10016

Routledge
Taylor & Francis Group
27 Church Road
Hove, East Sussex BN3 2FA

© 2011 by Taylor and Francis Group, LLC
Routledge is an imprint of Taylor & Francis Group, an Informa business

Printed in the United States of America on acid-free paper
10 9 8 7 6 5 4 3 2 1

International Standard Book Number: 978-0-415-88486-0 (Hardback) 978-0-415-88487-7 (Paperback)

Library of Congress Cataloging-in-Publication Data

With culture in mind : psychoanalytic stories / edited by Muriel Dimen.
    p. cm. -- (The relational perspectives book series ; vol. 50)
    Includes bibliographical references and index.
    ISBN 978-0-415-88486-0 (hardcover : alk. paper) -- ISBN 978-0-415-88487-7 (pbk. : alk. paper) -- ISBN 978-0-203-84066-5 (e-book)
    1. Object relations (Psychoanalysis) 2. Interpersonal relations. I. Dimen, Muriel.

BF175.5.O24W58 2011
150.19'5--dc22   2010045584

Visit the Taylor & Francis Web site at
http://www.taylorandfrancis.com

and the Routledge Web site at
http://www.routledgementalhealth.com

Contents

CONTENTS

Contributors

Jessica Benjamin, PhD, is a faculty member at the postdoctoral psychology program in psychotherapy and psychoanalysis at New York University. She is best known as the author of *The Bonds of Love: Psychoanalysis, Feminism and the Problem of Domination* (1988); her more recent books are *Like Subjects, Love Objects: Essays on Recognition and Sexual Difference* (1995) and *Shadow of the Other: Intersubjectivity and Gender in Psychoanalysis* (1997). Recently she has been writing on the idea of thirdness and on the problem of acknowledgment and mutual recognition. She is the director of The Acknowledgment Project, a dialogue project started in the Middle East between Israeli and Palestinian mental health professionals. She has lectured and supervised all over the world, presenting her perspective on the development of gender and intersubjectivity as well as on the clinical and social implications of acknowledgment. She helped to found *Studies in Gender and Sexuality* and the International Association for Relational Psychoanalysis and Psychotherapy. She is an associate editor of *Psychoanalytic Dialogues* and is also a cofounder and board member of the Stephen A. Mitchell Center for Relational Studies in New York. She is a psychoanalyst in private practice in New York City.

Muriel Dimen, PhD, is an adjunct clinical professor of psychology at New York University's (NYU's) postdoctoral program in psychotherapy and psychoanalysis and professor emerita of anthropology at Lehman College (CUNY). On the faculties of many institutes, she is editor of *Studies in Gender and Sexuality*, associate editor of *Psychoanalytic Dialogues*, and founding board member and former treasurer of the International Association for Relational Psychoanalysis and Psychotherapy. Her most recent book, *Sexuality, Intimacy, Power*, received the Goethe Award from the Canadian Psychological Association for the Best Book of Psychoanalytic Scholarship published in 2003. She has also written *Surviving Sexual Contradictions* (1986) and *The Anthropological Imagination* (1977). Her coedited books are *Gender in Psychoanalytic Space: Between Clinic and Culture* with Virginia Goldner (2002), *Storms in Her Head: New Clinical and Theoretical Perspectives on Breuer and Freud's Studies on Hysteria* with Adrienne Harris (2001), and *Regional Variation in Modern Greece and Cyprus: Toward an Ethnography of Greece* with Ernestine Friedl (1976). A fellow at the New York Institute for the Humanities at NYU, she practices in Manhattan and supervises nationally.

Orna Guralnik, PsyD, is an adjunct assistant professor in the Department of Psychology at New York University and is on the faculty of the National Institute for the Psychotherapies. She is cofounder of the Dissociative Disorders Research Center at Mount Sinai School of Medicine and is recipient of NARSAD, National Institutes of Health (NIH), and Wolstein grants. She teaches, presents, and publishes on the topic of dissociation, including the most recent "Standing in the Spaces Between Recognition and Interpellation" in *Psychoanalytic Dialogues*) (2010). Other writings include "Being and Having an Identity: Catherine Opie" (*Studies in Gender and Sexuality*, forthcoming). She is in private practice in New York City.

Stephen Hartman, PhD, is on the faculty of the Psychoanalytic Institute of Northern California, where he also cochairs the curriculum committee and sits on the board of directors. A graduate of the New York University postdoctoral program in psychotherapy and psychoanalysis, he is also on the faculty of the Steven A. Mitchell Center for Relational Psychoanalysis in New York City and the Northern California Society for Psychoanalytic Psychology and is contributing editor to *Studies in Gender and Sexuality* and assistant editor for *Psychoanalytic Dialogues*. He is the author of "Class Unconscious: From Dialectical Materialism to Relational Material" in *Relational Psychoanalysis, Vol. 3: New Voices* (2007) and "Reality 2.0: When Loss Is Lost" (*Psychoanalytic Dialogues*, forthcoming). He practices in New York and San Francisco, commuting via iChat.

Glenys Lobban, PhD, clinical psychologist and psychoanalyst, is a graduate of the New York University postdoctoral program in psychotherapy and psychoanalysis and adjunct clinical supervisor in the graduate program in clinical psychology at City University of New York (CUNY). Her "Immigration and Dissociation" appeared in *Psychoanalytic Perspectives* (2006), and she contributed a chapter to *Psychoanalytic Reflections on Deaths and Endings: Finality, Transformations, New Beginnings* (2007). She is in private practice in New York City with adults, adolescents, and couples.

Susie Orbach, PhD, is a psychoanalyst and writer. She cofounded The Women's Therapy Centre in London in 1976 and The Women's Therapy Centre Institute in New York in 1981. Her numerous publications include the classic *Fat Is a Feminist Issue* (1978), along with other such influential texts as *Hunger Strike* (2000), *The Impossibility of Sex* (2000), and the recently published *Bodies* (2009). She is a founder member of ANTIDOTE (working for emotional literacy) and Psychotherapists and Counsellors for Social Responsibility and is convener of Anybody (www.any-body.org), an organization campaigning for body diversity. She currently chairs the Relational School in the United Kingdom and has a clinical practice seeing individuals and couples.

Olga Pugachevsky, PhD, has presented at several national and international conferences. Her article, "A Lawyer Walks Into a Psychologist's Office," was published in *ONEonONE*, a publication of the General Practice Section of New York State Bar Association (fall 2009). She is a licensed clinical psychologist in private practice in New York.

Eyal Rozmarin, PhD, is a candidate at New York University's postdoctoral program in psychotherapy and psychoanalysis and a contributing editor at *Studies in Gender and Sexuality*. His recent work focuses on the intersection of psychoanalysis, critical theory, and philosophy. His publications include "I Am Yourself: Subjectivity and the Collective" (*Psychoanalytic Dialogues*, 2009), "David and Jonathan" (in *Heterosexual Masculinities: Contemporary Perspectives From Psychoanalytic Gender Theory*, 2009), and "An Other in Psychoanalysis; Lévinas' Critique of Knowledge and Analytic Sense" (*Contemporary Psychoanalysis*, 2007). He is in private practice in New York City.

Avgi Saketopoulou, PhD, is a candidate at New York University's postdoctoral program in psychotherapy and psychoanalysis. She is faculty at the Institute for Contemporary Psychotherapy and the Bronx Children's Psychiatric Center. Her writings include "The Therapeutic Alliance in Psychodynamic Psychotherapy: Theoretical Conceptualizations and Research Findings" (*Psychotherapy*, 1999), "Identifications Annealed, Adhesive and Political: Nina Farhi's Milner, Marion Milner's Susan" (*Psychoanalytic Dialogues*, 2010), "Minding the Gap: Race and Class in Clinical Work with Transgender Children" (*Psychoanalytic Dialogues*, 2011), and "Catherine Opie: American Photographer, American Pervert" (*Studies in Gender and Sexuality*, forthcoming). She is in private practice in New York City.

Andrew Samuels, PhD, is a professor of analytical psychology at Essex and holds visiting chairs at New York, Goldsmiths, and Roehampton. He is a Jungian Training Analyst and works internationally as a political consultant. He is chair of the United UK Council for Psychotherapy, founding board member of the International Association for Relational Psychoanalysis and Psychotherapy, and cofounder of Psychotherapists and Counselors for Social Responsibility (UK). His books have been translated into 19 languages and include *The Plural Psyche* (1989), *The Political Psyche* (1993), and the award-winning *Politics on the Couch* (2007). He is known for his work on the links between psychology and psychotherapy and sociopolitical problems, working with political material in the clinical session, sex, gender and relationships, masculinity and the father, and progressive spiritualities. He is in private practice in London.

Maura Sheehy, LCSW, runs a weekly support group for new mothers and their babies. She is the author of several papers on the issues of maternal identity formation and maternal subjectivity. Her most recent paper, "Manifesto for the Hybrid: Towards an Antidote to the Mother Discourse," was presented at the M(o)ther Trouble Conference in Birkbeck, University of London in 2009. As a magazine staff and freelance writer she has written extensively on politics, culture, parenting, and attachment for numerous magazines. She is a psychotherapist in private practice in Brooklyn, New York.

INTRODUCTION

MURIEL DIMEN

The chapters that follow constitute an experiment in form, voice, and vision. The experiment arose by happenstance. For several years, I have been leading a writing group for psychoanalysts; some are still in training, and others have been in practice for many years. The group took shape through several processes. It began as a reading group with a changing cast of characters. When, finally, it was clear that a core was hanging in through the years, the notion somehow emerged—we do not recall how—to move from reading together to writing. Word of the group spread, and by the end of another academic year a quorum of six had established itself. Give or take another year or two of settling in, as old hands moved on and new folks joined, and then one of the group, Stephen Hartman, suggested we work on a set of papers that could be presented as a panel at our annual conference.

Our process, which endures, was to address one member's work at a time. Each week, one writer would be on deck and would distribute the work digitally with sufficient time for all the rest to read it. At our weekly 1-hour meeting, we would ask the presenter how we could be of help; depending on need, we might spend 2 weeks, or even up to a month, on a single piece of writing, revisions of which might show up once or twice later on. From the beginning, I had levied only one rule: It was our job to help whomever was up to do what he or she wanted. What mattered was not what *we* thought should be written but how we could use our responses to help *the author* realize the goals of that particular piece of writing. I believed then, and still do, that it was crucial for us not to debate theory or clinical technique or politics. Our focus was literary, not professional. Certainly, given an author's aims, the group could then offer criticism: Taking the author's viewpoint, even if they disagreed with it, others in the group would articulate, from their distinct standpoints, the changes necessary to render the writer's argument convincing. This rather stringently applied policy—for the group spans clear, even sharp differences on questions of theory and clinical work, politics and values—has, in my view, allowed a remarkably varied range of unique voices to emerge.

As the group worked together, a shared set of intellectual concerns cohered at the intersection of their several backgrounds and interests: clinical writing, philosophy, critical theory, political science, art, journalism, and short-storytelling. From the members' diversity grew a mutually agreeable form: essays locating the psychic and the social in a single clinical moment. That moment might entail transference and countertransference or an enactment; a symptom or a facet of a personality; a newspaper headline or a cultural event or a war. Whatever the moment's content, it was to serve as opportunity and means to reflect on that familiar binary of mind versus culture, on the relationship between internal and external, psychic interior and sociopolitical surround.

This initial foray into this new model of psychoanalytic writing was a response to an occasion: the 2007 spring meeting of the American Psychological Association, Division of Psychoanalysis (39) in Toronto. This august context, however, levied what turned out to be a creative constraint: It allowed no more than 110 minutes for six papers plus introductions (I was to moderate) and audience discussion. So, in addition to tackling the relation between psyche and society, ever a moving target, the authors braved the challenge of distilling their accounts to 12–15 minutes each, that is, writing papers of 6–8 pages each (I am known for being strict also in equating one written page to 2 minutes' reading time, an equation various members of the group inevitably defied on occasion). Although some deliveries lasted somewhat longer than their allotted time (resulting, as is evident here, in papers of different lengths), still the whole appeared as a fascinating mosaic.

Indeed, audience discussion, even if cut a bit short by an embarrassment of intellectual, clinical, and literary riches, was sufficiently stimulating to generate ongoing interest in the work of this group of writers. So the group decided to take their show on the road and have been welcomed with open arms. The first batch of papers, here titled "The Social Third," was then given again, at two other venues: the International Association for Relational Psychoanalysis and Psychotherapy (IARPP), Athens, July 2007; and the Association for the Psychoanalysis of Culture and Society (APCS), Rutgers

University, October 2007. A new set of papers, "Interpellations," was prepared for Division 39 in New York City, April 2008. And a third set, "Subjective Experience, Collective Narratives," was delivered at IARPP, Tel Aviv, June 2009 and Division 39, Chicago, April 2010.

From these three sets of papers arose this book. Somewhere in 2008, as the group was preparing its 2009 panel, it occurred to me that we had a wonderful opportunity to offer a new way of talking about the analyst's struggle to grasp the patient's internal life as voiced in relation to others in their political, social, and material contexts. In retrospect, it has been important that this struggle found expression and debate in a collective context. Traditionally, psychoanalysts work in isolation from their colleagues. On a daily basis, they see their patients, one on one, in their consulting rooms and congregate for collegial exchange at the occasional lecture and conference. This group of writer-clinicians, however, has met for years, critiquing each other's essays (and, as an unintended by-product, helping each other in their clinical practices), which evolved and took their final form having marinated in this mutual exchange. As a result (and as on the panels), each essay in this book implicitly speaks to the others, rendering the ensuing conversation an infrastructure in which the 18 brief pieces weave a web of meaning about mind and culture.

What happened in the group is a microcosm of what is beginning to happen more widely in the psychoanalytic world. Analysts are acknowledging that the orthodox ways of analyzing people are insufficient. Usually analysts don't consider social forces. But these analysts, like the three well-known analysts who discuss the three sections into which the book is divided, do. Over time, they came to understand that their grasp of clinical problems needed more than the historical psychoanalytic focus on family narratives, patterns of relating, and attachment or sexual problems. In each case, they saw it made sense to consider psychoanalysis' conventional subject—interior life—as steeped in sociopolitical forces, that psychic life is made equally of inner and outer worlds, and they have found ways to talk about it that sacrifices neither dimension. Their novel approach, in turn, dovetails with a changing construal of clinical process.

The authors share this new paradigm's premise that intellectual and clinical practices are historical, linguistic, political, and contextual.

Likewise, they endorse its view of psychic structure (at least those aspects reachable by psychotherapy) as rooted in one's relations with other people. This reformulation of classical ideas does not dispense with a conception of an internal world as animated by forces different from those powering the external world; it offers instead an alternative to the traditional view that epigenetic drives shape the mind. The clinical work discussed in this book was conducted on the assumption that therapeutic action—and, hence, transformation—issues from the culturally situated and personally meaningful relationship that arises and evolves, and which is jointly explored, between patient and therapist.

With Culture in Mind explores what psychoanalysis is only now starting to get: Culture saturates subjective experience. Indeed, it is the business of psychoanalytic practice to document this approach to treatment. Through the process of their weekly meetings, the authors discovered they were as caught up in the cultural dynamics as their patients; in some way, the analyses had come to a halt, leaving the analysts feeling they lacked the tools to reach the particular patient. All were variously stuck within the bounds of discourse and ideology: those unconscious, received ways of thinking that prescribe and proscribe how we can think about ourselves. Using that insight, each writer-analyst independently generated a way out: to work toward making conscious the unconscious embroilment with social ideology they identified in their patients and themselves.

This book shows how seven practicing psychoanalysts, each in his or her own way, put this emergent psychoanalytic awareness into clinical practice. Each offers an account of an analyst–patient relationship that opens spaces for new clinical choices. In the therapeutic dyads described, the mind–society synapse fires, enabling a psychic–social moment to be formulated, addressed, and located in clinical time, revealing ever new ways to mean. But these dyads reckon with striking contextual twists, involving, for example, disability, gay marriage, immigration, emigration, racism, sexual prejudice, new communications technologies, genocide, and war. The authors enlist personal, artistic, and clinical experience, as well as psychoanalytic and social theory, to show how collective forces fuse to both generate and trouble the experience of individuals.

Here I want to frame these unusual, concise essays by naming a group of concepts critical to them. In the body of the book, I will introduce each chapter in turn, elaborating these ideas and also addressing the nexus of the authors' theoretical and literary, not to mention clinical, strategies. The authors' common point of view is that of critique, be it of psychoanalysis or clinical technique or society. In service of this stance, they employ a range of notions: interpellation; resignification; intelligibility; nationalism; the Third. Some of these concepts (e.g., "the Third") are current in psychoanalytic usage. Others (e.g., "interpellation" and "resignification") originate in contemporary cultural theory. And still others (e.g., "nationalism" or "intelligibility") straddle the divides of ordinary and disciplinary speech. Whether colloquial or not, however, these ideas are all used with a critical edge, which shows up implicitly or overtly, if differently, in each essay.

This critical stance is perhaps best described by the concept of "discourse," whose utility for us lies in its capacity to link the psychic and the social (Foucault, 1977). In critical theory, it may be defined as what delimits both how we think and how we think about how we think. The power of discourse lies in its exclusions, in what it overtly or implicitly tells us we may not think. Discursive formations, to put it differently, are power structures. They are networks of socially located ideas, beliefs, attitudes, behaviors, and action patterns that systematically fashion and inform subjectivity and its practices.

Every discipline operates with discursive power. Classical psychoanalysis, for example, tells us we may think about the mind but only in a particular way—the mind as we know it in an individual body. Implicitly excluded from that one-person model of mind is what has become a postclassical commonplace: mind as existing between bodies as well, that is, intersubjectivity. But, as these essays argue or demonstrate, even two-person psychologies may exclude other, necessary sources of knowledge, in particular, theories of the cultural and political construction of subjectivity.

One concept animating this project of critique is interpellation. Interpellation is a particularly strong instance of discourse's traffic in power, for it conveys the sense of danger in venturing into excluded territory. According to Louis Althusser (1971), a French structural Marxist analyzed by Jacques Lacan, interpellation names the (political) process by which subjectivity is hailed into being. Althusser's emblematic model for it is what happens when, upon hearing a police officer on the street call "Hey, you!" you turn around. The imagery is intentional: Subjectivity as a state of being is said to be authorized by the Law (*le nom du père*, in Lacanian terms) or, what is the same, by the prevailing discourse. It comes to us from outside, from the top down, from everywhere and anywhere. And without it we would be nowhere.

As appears in some of these essays, interpellation implies "intelligibility" (Butler, 2000/1990). A psychosocial concept par excellence, it attempts to address the classic conundrum of domination: How does it come about that we collude in our own oppression? Interpellation, as an idea, argues that our collusion and our oppression are constructed of the same stuff. It entails a paradox: One becomes a subject of oneself, an autonomous and sovereign being, only by becoming subject to the Law's sovereignty, to discourse, or to society itself. In other words, one becomes auth-entic—intelligible to oneself—only by recognizing the auth-ority of discourse to render one's being intelligible. Even before one comes into being, one is always already constructed as a subject: Even before birth, for example, parents-to-be will imagine relations with that other subject, now a fetus who, once born, will be their child and is, and will be, intelligible only as a separate center of subjectivity-to-be. If intelligibility is also key to integrity and sanity, however, one's freedom and capacity to change depend on "resignification," on the capacity to endow old enchainments with new meaning—which one may define as a principal goal of psychoanalysis, not to mention struggles for political and cultural liberation.

This book divides into three parts: "The Social Third," "Interpellations," and "Subjective Experience, Collective Narratives." Each essay—by Orna Guralnik, Stephen Hartman, Glenys Lobban, Olga Pugachevsky, Eyal Rozmarin, Avgi Saketopoulou, and Maura Sheehy—is prefaced by a very brief introduction articulating its goals and relation to the whole. And each part concludes with a discussion by analysts well known for their writing about mind and society—Jessica Benjamin, Susie Orbach, and Andrew Samuels.

We are honored by the willingness of these distinguished thinkers to contribute to this project—to, in effect, the next generation's work. Their voices are likewise varied, and their traditions and discourses cover a fine range; sometimes they admire the essays they discuss, sometimes they are puzzled, sometimes they flat-out disagree. My hope is that their praise, assessments, challenges, and reflections will both speak to readers' responses and stir even more questions.

Of the three, Benjamin inhabits the same part of the psychoanalytic world as the authors. One of the prime architects of relational psychoanalysis and now turning this body of thought to engaged political use, she focuses her commentary on the clinical situation. Drawing on her grounding in philosophy, social theory, and psychoanalytic feminist thought, she aims "to highlight what is gained or lost or made more troublesome by admitting the intensity of interpellation our psychoanalyst authors allow themselves to experience."

Orbach, likewise a pioneer of feminist psychoanalysis, recalls other classic engagements between psychoanalysis and social thought, from Wilhelm Reich to Franz Fanon. "Addressing cultural familial intrapsychic and inter-psychic pressures is," she says, "what we do," a purpose, she argues when taking issue with some of the authors, not always well served by postmodernism. From an overview of her own history on the New Left and in the women's movement, she conveys how she, jointly with colleagues, treats the nexus of mind and society.

With drama, Samuels writes a letter to each of the authors, his questions putting a new spin on their offerings. Characteristically concerned to locate the political and the clinical in each other, he not only asks whether a common experience of citizenship couches the therapeutic dyad, but he also wonders whether this political truth in fact makes unconscious communication possible at all. "If this is the case, then what has been located behind the corral fence of the taboo on politics within psychoanalysis has been secretly facilitating our work all along."

Whatever their particular perspective, these three essays, like the chapters they discuss, work at once on three different levels: the clinical moment where mind and society meet; the critique of social and psychoanalytic theory; and the assessment of social forces. *With Culture in Mind: Psychoanalytic Stories* reveals the power of a culturally informed psychotherapy: analysts and patients alike can change their lives if they confront the cultural–psychological impasses in which they find themselves.

PART I
THE SOCIAL THIRD

1

MELISSA

Lost in a Fog, or "How Difficult Is This MOMMY Stuff, Anyway?"

MAURA SHEEHY

EDITOR'S INTRODUCTION

There is a socially pervasive struggle with intelligibility and abjection that is most often theorized, as it is later in this book, in regard to the sexual sphere. However, as Maura Sheehy recounts, it is also at home in familial and personal life. Here the analyst works with Melissa, a young mother, who, just like her analyst, struggles with the multiple interpellations of motherhood, its idealization and abjection producing both exaltation and utter confused misery. As we read, we witness a parallel process in which the analyst finds and sees how both her patient and she locate themselves in and wrestle with discourse, a process that effects change in both.

Melissa began our first session perched on the edge of the couch and turned toward me at an uncomfortable angle, leaving herself both unsupported and off balance. She had two daughters, she said, ages 3½ years and 8 months, and was feeling sad and overwhelmed due to what she assumed were "postpartum weaning issues." She said she was sorry to be giving up the symbiotic breast-feeding connection with her infant but also glad to be freed up from the constant nursing demands. Rather than enjoying her new freedom, however, she felt panic and loss. "They're growing up, I haven't done the baby books, I'm not recording what's happening, my older daughter never talks to me about herself, it's all slipping away," she said, tearing up.

Simultaneously, she felt she should be getting back to work. An Ivy League educated architect, Melissa had designed and directed the building of their whole apartment while pregnant and now expected herself to perform a similar virtuosity of multitasking. But she couldn't finish even the tiny lobby design she'd been hired to do by her co-op board and felt a mounting sense of failure and shame. She wondered if she could ever return to architecture after seeing the angry, viciously competitive older women at the firms she'd worked at, who never saw their families. She wondered why she couldn't find a way to balance her life "like everyone else."

Everything in Melissa's life seemed to be where it was by default rather than choice. Chaos reigned. Despite having a full-time babysitter she was often late to sessions, having been derailed by some relative trifle like her daughter's tantrumy mind changes about who would take her to school. She longed for time to herself but couldn't separate for fear her girls would suffer somehow, but if she did break away she busied herself with mindless chores. When she did spend time with her children it never seemed terribly satisfying, despite her initial complaint, because she was so anxious about how the interactions and activities should go. She admitted that sometimes the babysitter's presence made her feel "like I'm on an IV [intravenous] drip in the back room," but nevertheless the babysitter was omnipresent, even at the, in their case, not-just-mommy-and-me classes. Yet every night she was bedeviled by the thought: "What do I need to do tomorrow to be a good parent?"

Melissa felt a general sense of exile in motherhood, as if she'd been dismissed from the world and was like "a peg that didn't fit." She imagined her former colleagues assuming she "couldn't hack it" and snickering at her retreat into motherhood, the co-op board laughing at the little mother who couldn't get the job done, and the ultra-trendy professionals in her neighborhood greeting her stroller-pushing presence with a disapproving "what are YOU doing here?" But she couldn't connect with the other preschool mothers for fear of what they'd think once they found out she had a full-time babysitter, house cleaner, and a SoHo loft, and wasn't working—again, she'd be dismissed. Above all, she felt she had no right to complain—about anything. As her husband asked whenever she voiced a need, she imagined everyone wondering, "What do you DO all day?"

I was struck by Melissa's near-complete lostness—as if she could not find comfort in any part of her identity or the world—and her lack of definition was evident in her wandering, overgeneralized, contradictory associations. She felt "lost in a fog," and so did I. Nothing we did seemed to get at what was really "slipping away" or to provide much relief. And then I began to dismiss her, too. After all, she was easy to dismiss: a wealthy, White, educated, stylish woman, rolling in help and lost in an abundance of options. Were the voices of censure that bedeviled her not somehow deserved, not perhaps a symptom of her privilege?

My fantasies of a meaty attachment-related analysis devolved into disappointment as once again she brought in one of the self-help/parenting books she studied hungrily and recited their simple revelations. Our sessions began to feel like mommy coaching 101, and my mind became cluttered with reductive prescriptions such as, "She needs to cut back on that babysitter so she can feel more connected to her kids, and then we'll help her get back to work part-time." Impatiently, dismissively, I kept wondering, "Where is the second-time mother with her game in place; why can't she get control of those kids, set the schedule, send her sitter on errands, do what she wants?" As I reflected on what was at the base of my impatience, I heard a voice say, "How difficult IS this MOMMY stuff, anyway?"

Dimly, I was aware that something about this reaction was off. All my own mother chaos, ambivalence, trouble balancing all the desires and needs—my own and my children's—was disavowed. My confidence wavered. I couldn't stop wondering if I was reacting to her as a mother or analyst (and what exactly the difference might be), prescribing my own biased cures or meeting her needs. The identifications and disidentifications were disorienting. I was back to work only 4 months since having my second child and felt my mother self to be barely hidden behind a too-shaky hologram of my analyst self. It felt reductive to be thinking of her, and myself, at such a binary dead end, in terms of a self that was independent, separate from children, and defined by work, or as a mother self, as if it were possible to separate our desire and identities into neat piles. I felt stuck but could not see what I was stuck in. So I resolved for a while to examine her history more closely—an analytic fallback position, to be sure, but somewhere that I hoped would anchor us.

As we peeled back the historical layers we found the mother who was a poster child for pre-feminist domestic enslavement and the father who was a first-generation immigrant grooming Melissa for greatness, teaching her to leave play for after work and to be anything but her mother. Her early talent for painting had been immediately commodified into a product to be bought by her father or his friends and then pushed aside for "real" work. But the work was never done, until she finished graduate school and realized the mountain she'd climbed to the cutting-edge career "was really," she said, "just a cliff" that led to more endless work, no play, no time for family. Now she feared she'd pour herself in to her daughters and they would use her up like a commodity, then eventually dismissing her as everyone else in the world did.

Around this time, I wrote an essay for a writing group of analysts exploring my own conflicts over separation from and connection with my children, my heated desire for both, and the elemental fears that could arise from either state during the course of a day. I related my search through the attachment, object relations, and relational canons to find something that spoke to MY experience—MY maternal identity—rather than only my effect on my child and my child's maternal experience. To my utter surprise, someone said they didn't get why I had to read books at all, why didn't I just know what I wanted and then do it? It was the voice I'd heard in myself in response to Melissa, now coming from outside: "How difficult is this MOMMY stuff, anyway?" Mothers were supposed to KNOW how to manage motherhood, not flip around like a fish out of water or talk about their own desire. While writing I had noticed the feeling that revealing my mother self felt humiliating and inappropriate outside the home sphere, not worthy of intellectual inquiry, just mommy talk, mommy crap. Now it seemed confirmed, and as I went home suffused in shame I felt a sudden surge of identification with Melissa. As Melissa and I answered society's hailing as mothers, had we, as Judith Butler (1993) suggested, taken our new, maternal identity in as a "reprimand" that had repressed other parts of ourselves in return for offering us recognition as mothers?

Still seeking to clean up my countertransference and return to some supposed "solid" analytic stance toward Melissa, I brought Melissa's case to an all-female supervision group. To my surprise, they reacted to the case with pained anxiety and identification with the patient as all their unresolved conflicts about their work and motherhood choices and their shifting sense of their own subjectivity surfaced. I began to see how filled we were with negative maternal images and impossible expectations of ourselves, how little we understood the forces at work upon and within us, how we blamed ourselves for our own confusion and inability to find balance, thinking we had so many choices. But did we?

According to a Harvard University study by the Project for Global Working Families, out of 173 countries the United States is one of five that doesn't provide paid maternity leave (Heymann, Earle, & Hayes, 2007). The others are Lesotho, Swaziland, Liberia, and Papua New Guinea. And our access to basic supports such as family sick leave, national child-care standards, and affordable health-care coverage not tied to a full-time job lag far behind those of most developed countries. Judy Warner, in her book *Perfect Madness* (2005), made a strident argument that the lack of social policy supporting families has made it impossible for women not to feel betrayed, as Melissa does, by the message that we can have it all—work and motherhood—and develop a fairly stable and positive maternal identity when in fact we can't, easily if at all.

But Melissa's case opened my eyes to an even more insidious set of internal obstacles to the development of a maternal subjectivity that includes a sense of agency. First, the tendency to think in binaries—work versus motherhood, good mother versus bad, separate versus connected. Reflecting and reproducing the bifurcated social structure within which women try to be both workers and mothers, these binaries leave women without any psychic in-between territory for exploration or creation of a maternal subjectivity that doesn't, still, contain shame.

Melissa's personal financial and class advantages had blinded me to the more universal conflicts she and I were caught in and had anesthetized me to her real anguish. But as we unpacked her maternal shame,

I found my own. I had thought myself very different from her, less ambivalent about my delight in the maternal experience. But there I was, feeling my maternal identity was something to hide and wanting to solve her confusion as it reminded me too painfully of my own. I realized how lost I was in the confusing web of social constructions of women and mothers that no amount of feminist reading or conscious-ness raising had been able to free me from, despite how enlightened, and therefore immune, I had thought myself.

I began to wonder about this self-hating mother introject and how it prevents women from taking their own maternal desire seriously. By maternal desire I mean not only what Daphne de Marneffe (2004) called the profound, drive-like need to have physical and emotional contact with one's children but also our maternal subjectivity in the larger sense—who we become and what we desire for ourselves when we become mothers. There is almost no way to think about ourselves as having aching desires for deeply intimate relationships with our children while also remaining connected to the larger world and to ourselves. We are taught to think about ourselves only in two abso-lutely opposed categories: as maternal facilitators and holders who can have no desire but to respond to our children's needs and not our own; or as women who can clearly and consistently individuate away from the maternal role (which, we are told, is good for us and them). But individuate too much, desire too much in either direction, and one is a bad mother: engulfing, engulfed, regressed, or too separate.

I no longer felt that our conversations about motherhood texts were beside the point. After all, where else was discussion of a mother's experience to be found but in those steerage class, self-help regions of the bookstore, or in the work, usually memoir, of women writ-ing from and about the same binary- and shame-defined confines we were stuck in. I also didn't cringe when Melissa saw an article I'd written for *Child* magazine (Sheehy, 2004), in which I revealed some of my messy maternal process, or when my bag tipped over and a sea of Cheerios skittered across the floor, or when she asked me how I'd figured it all out. "What makes you think I have?" I answered. "I'm struggling too, doing what you are: reading, talking with other moth-ers, looking for mentors and models. There is no other way."

One night around this time Melissa went to hear a panel of artists discuss their process, and the next day she came to session feeling inspired to resume her painting. Then she announced triumphantly that she knew why her oldest daughter wasn't sharing anything about herself: "I'm not talking to her about my process, my secrets!" said Melissa, "so she's not talking to me about hers." I was struck by Melissa's use of the evening's gift and my decision to share my maternal "secrets." She wasn't just following the healthy development script of Mother separating from her children to fulfill herself, finding identity in separation and individuation. Rather, in finding more of her own voice she found more of a voice as a mother, too—the parts of herself not opposed in a binary, but intertwined.

2

DARREN AND STEPHEN

Erotic Interludes in Political Transference

STEPHEN HARTMAN

EDITOR'S INTRODUCTION

The concept of interpellation is enhanced when we add to it Judith Butler's (2000/1990) concept of intelligibility, which she theorizes as key to subjectivity because it is what permits recognition. In "Darren and Stephen: Erotic Interludes in Political Transference," Stephen Hartman shows how interpellation makes both him and Darren intelligible and therefore anxious: The power of discourse to legitimate desire means that you can lose your legitimacy and fall into abjection if you ever refuse your interpellation. Here Hartman, interpellated by the *New York Times* announcement of his marriage to another man, desexualizes and abjects his patient by interpellating his desire as a desire to be a married gay guy, a "good gay" too.

Darren bursts into my office 10 minutes late: 10 minutes I have grown to anticipate. I usually take the moment to scan the headlines. Today's news is grim. The New York State Court of Appeals has ruled that gays have no rational, constitutional right to marry. I am scowling as Darren saunters by. Not noticing, or trying not to notice, he offers a quick, anemic "Hey!" and sprawls on his chair as if unfolding on a hammock. Then a look to reprimand: "Come on, already, put the fucking newspaper down; let's get on with it." His arms are crossed above his head, and his biceps peek out of an unseasonable polo shirt, flexed for me to enjoy.

Darren makes no bones about wanting to turn me on. He is lean and sexy but not so appealing to me because he is plaintive and a tad desperate in his seductive overtures. I assume that he approaches other men with the same flirt and destroy, which I take to explain why he has an easy time getting laid but a hellish time finding a boyfriend. Until this session, I hadn't fully grasped the way Darren falls back in his chair. His biceps ride up past his ears where his feet want to go: The gesture contains a wish as dangerous as Darren's wish to surrender emotionally, the wish to be intelligible as a man who takes another man into him.

I don't consider Darren's sexual pleasure when I say that I like him very much. I imagine him as a man I could take as a peer, not a partner I could take in more carnal ways. We would be friends in another life. Perhaps in the life that Darren read about in the *New York Times* when my boyfriend, Henry, and I were married. There it was in print: We were interpellated "good gays," gentlemen with Princeton educations—our class struggles as obscure as our rowdiest fucking. The *Times* rejected a slightly racy picture of Henry spooning me from behind in favor of the eyebrows at the same level, life-partner look. We were presented with a storybook gay life to match Darren's parents' storybook Connecticut marriage: ours imagined among A-list gays who trade in design hotels and Rainbow fundraisers; theirs supplemented by a pack of healthy children, well mannered and well educated, bred during long nights of athletic, hetero-normal sex, Darren figures, telling me repeatedly about the banging of the headboard on the primal party wall.

That Darren's fantasy of marital bliss is, to say the least, idealized, we know. Much of our work focuses on the way idealization breathes eros into a hopelessly depressed father hiding the night away in his office, libidinizes a resentful exhausted mother, and stations Darren in the role of arbitrator between dueling parents to ensure they present a Town and Country façade. And me: still working at this unglamorously late hour. No headboard banging for this hard-working gay. And something very important missed about Darren. Marriage is not only lace curtains and tender lovemaking. If I could marry Darren, I could have him on his knees, and if I could give him the thrill of servicing me, I could also destroy him by naming him the fag. Cleansed by the bright hope of gay marriage, Darren and I had allowed the darkest timbres in the conjugal aria to elude us. Imagine being able to tolerate binding the most degenerate sex with the surest love? Darren can't. We haven't. I am, for Darren, married, and he is, for me, a patient.

Something is off today, though. Not the faux-affirmative, "we play on the same team" kick-off, this round. Darren gets right down to the scrimmage where our sessions typically end—looks like teammates even though I kicked him in the knee to steal the ball. No boasting about the latest Latin. Darren is pissed about his paltry share of romance, and once again caring for others.

Darren is chronically single. Our conversation turns to a long list of the men he has sex with who don't measure up to partner status. This one is a hopeless bottom. That one has no career prospects. Along comes Mr. Appropriate, and "pfffwt!" Darren traces the arc of a fizzling erection. There is no me to introduce to his family. Darren is not as lucky as I am, he sneers, and explains that it is easy for me to be smug with my "quote unquote boyfriend."

(Henry and I still use the term "boyfriend," not "husband," and we try to avoid the term "partner"—though it is a fallback in tricky professional situations. We want to preserve the feeling of romance that binds us and the sexual possibility that preserves our romance after many years.)

"My quote unquote boyfriend?" I ask a bit confused.

"Don't call him your boyfriend; he's your husband! Why do you use the term boyfriend anyway? You want everyone to think you have everything—" He clips his words.

"Go on," I encourage.

"You can't be in the *Times* and carry on like queers on the make! You and Henry were flirting all over the room at the Black Party. You pretend to be married, but it's a joke. I have to come in here and pretend that you have a perfect relationship so I can imagine having one for myself. Dr. Good Gay and his fabulous boyfriend. The whole situation sucks and I lose."

I don't say that Darren has homed in on my worst fear about analytic authority: that I might be normalized through my patient's identification. Have I self-servingly bought into Darren's idealization of a life I don't exactly lead? And on a day when I feel more knocked down than I realize? I struggle with feeling fraudulent in this self-state and worry that my effort to work through a positive transference is a front for my wish to be normal. Perhaps, ashamed of my own sexual greed, I desexualize Darren. It is all too easy to do: Cleansed by marriage, he and I enact a social dictate to button up our 501s and put our feet back on the ground.

We sit quietly for a bit, but Darren's not done. He lets it rip. "You think you're one of the good-fucking gays," he sneers and continues on and on once again pushing all the weight of the gay but-not-fucking world up happily married hill.

"What's that anyway?" I ask carefully not wanting to deny his rage. "I mean what exactly is a 'good fucking gay' on a day like this?" suddenly conscious of the headline that kicked off our session.

"Fuck!" he exclaims as we both begin to laugh, "We're screwed!"

"Or not!"

"I get wrapped up in what I imagine about you or my parents because it makes me feel I could have someone special for myself. But then something like this happens, and it's just hopeless. If I keep having sex with the sketchy boys I like, I'll never marry a respectable guy like you! Now I can't even get married! I come in here and elevate you to convince myself I am respectable. It hurts me. I am always chasing after you and never finding a guy who excites me. The reality is that you're not 'married' either. I mean, not in the way we want to believe."

I'm in my theory head, wanting to explain that regulatory discourse outside the session has limited our ability to fully use the transference. The dangling carrot of marriage had given Darren a gold standard for envy and rendered us intelligible so long as we play normal. Deferred was the opportunity for Darren to allow an inappropriate man, a man who would hold Darren's feet over his head, to be trustworthy and make him feel respected. Perhaps now, both declared inappropriate for marriage, our transference can endure this erotic wish.

"We got thrown off course," I begin. "It makes me think about the way our sessions go. It starts out flirty but respectable. We talk about how you want to marry a guy like me, and it ends up with you envious and angry that I disappoint you."

"I feel obligated to make you feel respectable," he admits. "It humiliates me. I idealize you—and I'm the one making you idealizable."

Impressed by his candor, I continue: "We never wonder what might be exciting about my humiliating you, or how that part of what makes a lover hot also makes a man unworthy of respect. (pause) I've noticed that when a guy says he loves you, you react as though he were putting you in an untenable position, crushing your desire while demanding that you service him."

"I get frightened that he'll crumble. At some point, he'll get needy. Maybe he'll turn against me the way my father would when he couldn't compete with me, or maybe I'll just end up taking care of him but not getting much in return."

"Yeah, but just maybe, you're excited by the risk? However you feel about my need to feel married, whatever you have to do to make me feel married, I think you like the idea that I could be nasty and still trustworthy. But, if you found a man like that, it might feel too much like your mother: pretending to have a perfect marriage while feeling submissive and disrespected. So you don't take the risk. You trade in wanting to be sexual for wanting to be respectable. We need to understand why you can't have both."

"I'm still in that self-effacing role with my family," he observes, "and somehow I can't stop wanting that role with you ... wanting to build you up and then feel ashamed of it." We wonder if servicing others is a gay curse: You yield desire to be the best little boy in the world and think you've hit the lotto when the *New York Times* determines that your life is fit to print.

3

Lɪ-ᴀɴ

Wounded by War

GLENYS LOBBAN

EDITOR'S INTRODUCTION

These clinical vignettes illustrate the power of discourse and how patients and analysts alike get lost in it. This may sound like enactment or transference and countertransference. But we are saying that there is also a Third in the room—the politics of mental health and illness, of race, gender, and sex, of psychoanalysis. Here, Glenys Lobban tells of her work with a Vietnamese immigrant in which her countertransference is inflected by discourse or, more precisely, by a denial of it, and an enactment facilitates not only the analyst's recognition of her countertransference blindness but the patient's capacity to resignify her experience.

Li-an arrived at our first session dressed all in black, wearing a short skirt and tights. She sported a punk haircut and many piercings. She told me her story, which was filled with trauma and violence, in a soft, melodious voice. She seemed tentative and eager to please.

Li-an is the oldest daughter of middle-class Vietnamese refugees. Her father was a senior officer in the South Vietnamese military and her mother was a socialite. Li-an recalls that the atmosphere in her home in Saigon was calm; there were no explosive outbursts of parental anger despite the bombs outside. Li-an was 3 years old when her family boarded an American helicopter and flew out of Saigon, just before it fell, leaving their house and their possessions behind. The family entered a refugee camp in Florida. A year later they moved to a small, predominantly White, Texan town, where they were the only Vietnamese family and the only Buddhists. Li-an's parents had to take menial jobs because they did not speak much English; her mother cleaned houses and her father worked on a production line in a factory. Many young men in their Texan town had died in Vietnam. Their new neighbors seemed to blame Li-an's family for the whole Vietnam debacle and saw them as the "enemy," in spite of the fact that her father fought alongside the Americans. They were often taunted or spurned, and local adolescents painted racist slogans on their house.

Her parents were homesick and depressed in Texas. Her father felt humiliated and defeated, a failure in war and in his job. Her mother hated being a domestic worker and angrily blamed her husband for their deprivations. They brought the war with them to Texas and reproduced it at home. Li-an recalls that the interactions between her parents were often full of explosive anger. Her parents also took out their frustration on Li-an. At age 9, Li-an cooked dinner and babysat her four younger siblings every day after school, yet her mother constantly accused Li-an of being "lazy" and "spoiled." Li-an was beaten by her parents for being "sneaky" and "untrustworthy." She internalized her mother's accusations and distrusted herself. When she entered therapy she believed that she was a "bad" person who possessed a potential for evil.

Out in the world, Li-an behaved as if she were in the midst of a minefield. With strangers she anticipated criticism, rapidly became defensive, and frequently got into arguments. Her intimate relationships became battlegrounds, because she tended to choose lovers and friends who were very critical of her and attacked her verbally or physically, while she sought to appease them.

After hearing about Li-an's life one might predict that she would bring the war at home to my office and that some kind of battle would take place between Li-an and myself. Well she did bring the war with her, but only indirectly, and she never, ever, got angry with me. Li-an brought precipitates of the war at home to our sessions—her pain and sadness and her sense that she was "totally unimportant." Often war would break out between sessions, and she'd call me because she felt desperately depressed or fragmented, following an interaction with a parent, lover, or coworker.

Li-an started to write a novel about a Vietnamese refugee family shortly before she began treatment. She shared her writing with me as the treatment and the novel progressed, and this formed the backbone of our work together. When she wrote about the fictional family, memories from her childhood erupted, and we processed them. Her writing was slow and painful, and we'd examine why she was blocked and what she was afraid to remember. She gradually accessed her anger at her parents and expressed it to me. She felt very disloyal when she finally described her parents' abuse, because she was deeply attached to them and sympathized with their plight as refugees. She believed that her father and mother were wounded by war and that this was the etiology of their verbally and physically abusive behavior during her childhood. After about 3 years in treatment, Li-an confronted her parents and told them that they had misjudged and mistreated her. She informed them that she had decided to "go public" and include a character in her novel who was abused by her parents. By the time our work together ended, Li-an had achieved what Judith Butler (1997) terms "resignification" (p. 105). She ceased to label herself as "bad" and "deserving of punishment," her self definition broadened, and she no longer only saw herself through her mother's lens.

What made these changes possible? I will describe some important clinical moments. Initially, Li-an and I co-constructed a neutral zone where we could experience and reflect on the war outside. Neither of us was consciously aware that the neutral zone had come into being or of the needs it served until late in the treatment.

It happens that my father, like Li-an's father, was psychically wounded by war. He was a gentle, peaceable soul, an idealist who volunteered to fight Adolf Hitler in World War II. He was captured in Egypt and spent 4 traumatic years as a prisoner of war in a camp run by the Germans. After the war he developed amnesia and was unable to remember the events of the 6 months he spent in England while waiting for transport back to South Africa. My parents met and married shortly after my father returned from the war, and I was born a year later. My father became depressed and distant periodically during my childhood. Like Li-an, I assumed that my father's emotional difficulties were the result of his war wounds, and like Li-an I registered my father's pain viscerally and wished to magically dissolve and repair it. Our parallel experiences with war wounds served as a backdrop for the neutral zone we co-constructed. I decided to make this backdrop more explicit after Li-an asked me to read and comment on a first draft of her novel. I told her a brief version of my father's story and my wish to heal his wounds. I decided to reveal this information because I felt it would be a relief to Li-an to know that we had shared similar experiences. I waited to reveal my experiences until she had a clear idea about her novel's plot and content and a finished first draft.

Li-an and I coexisted and the treatment progressed apace in our neutral zone for some years. Then one day the neutral zone was breached when Li-an arrived at my office in a state of a great excitement. Her publisher had hatched a plan for a public relations exercise. He offered to fund a trip to Vietnam for Li-an and her parents. It would be her father's first return visit to his country since the end of the war and Li-an's opportunity to reunite her father with his estranged sister in Vietnam. The sister, who was a nurse with the Viet Cong, had remained in Vietnam after the war, and the siblings had not spoken since. Li-an had made contact with her father's sister on a previous visit to Vietnam. The whole trip would be videotaped by a reporter and used to market Li-an's novel.

This plan dovetailed neatly with Li-an's wish to repair her parents' wounds. I had a very strong reaction to the plan. I felt that I could not support it and needed to speak out to protect Li-an. For the first time in the treatment, Li-an and I were in conflict. I was afraid that she would fail to effect reconciliation and heal her father's wounds and that this would lead her to feel distraught and destroyed. I was furious with her publisher for proposing such a risky, exploitative plan. I told Li-an that I was concerned that the reconciliation would fail, but I tried not to reveal the extent of my anxiety. The intensity of my response mystified me, so I discussed it with a colleague before our next session. My colleague and I gave my response a social read. We decided that Li-an's choice to go to Vietnam with her parents was based in a non-Western philosophical model that emphasizes interdependent selves (Harlem, 2009, p. 280) community, forgiveness, and reparation. I was trying to impose the traditional psychoanalytic (and of course Western) notion on Li-an that focused only on the individual and assumes a "normative independent self" (Harlem, 2009, p. 281). I was assuming that the individual can change only herself. When I unpacked all of this with my colleague, I was shocked that I had so readily accepted the role of the enforcer of Western and traditional psychoanalytic values. I viewed myself as "flexible" and "enlightened" and naively assumed that I was immune to the shaping power of discourse. I also realized that Li-an could have predicted that I would oppose her plan. She would often come back to New York after a visit home devastated by her parents' insensitivity, and I'd advise her: "You have to give up hoping your parents will change in order to protect yourself from disappointment." Li-an's second-generation, immigrant, raised-in-Texas self would agree with me, but another part of her continued to be committed to ideals of community and family.

The neutral zone we had co-constructed was based on the premise that our experiences were similar. To continue with the war metaphors, Li-an breached the neutral zone because she was ready to address our differences. She tossed a loaded gun to me to see what I'd do with it. Would I use it against her or allow her to choose a different path? Could I accept her values that privileged community or would I insist on branding them as pathological? In our next session I told Li-an I would support her whatever she decided to do. She said she had always planned to proceed with the plan to visit Vietnam no matter what I thought, but she was relieved that I was not opposing it.

In Vietnam the planned reconciliation took place. While the trip to Vietnam failed to heal all her father's wounds, he was deeply changed after his return to his homeland and his meeting with his sister. Li-an's relationship with him also improved. She joyfully described these changes to me when she returned. Over time Li-an and I discussed and processed our clash of cultures and parsed our differences and similarities.

When I began writing this chapter about Li-an, I had a startling experience. I flashed on a trip that my family took to England when I was 12 years old. It was my father's first visit back to England since his postwar amnesia. I understood something that had eluded me through all these years and that had never come up in my own analysis. I finally realized that I had harbored a hope that the trip to England would restore my father's memory and heal his war wounds. I think I felt more and more devastated as the trip progressed and this healing did not happen. Family lore is that I kept leaving shoes behind in every bed and breakfast we stayed in. Perhaps my missing shoes represented an attempt to alert myself, and my totally oblivious family, to the fact that something was lost and we should be seeking it.

So what should we privilege as we think about Li-an's plan to transport her father back to the scene of the crime? Should we privilege my social "clash of cultures," read on the causes of my anxiety about her plan? Should we privilege a personal read: that I feared she'd have her hopes dashed as I did? Or are they both equally valid and inextricably intertwined?

4

MARIANA

An MS Patient in My Office

OLGA PUGACHEVSKY

EDITOR'S INTRODUCTION

One problematic the writing group took up was the relationship between theoretical and clinical writing. Theory appears variously in these clinical vignettes. Sometimes it is addressed as such in the cases of Guralnik, Lobban, and Hartman. In other instances, it is seamlessly woven in, as in Sheehy's account or, next, in the deftly written vignette by Olga Pugachevsky. She narrates her work with Mariana, a patient, who, precociously accommodating and accomplished in projective identification, had acquired a chronic and progressive illness readily interpellatable by others—including the analyst—such that the patient is rendered an invalid, a subjectivity that both compels and repels her.

Mariana arrives at my office in her gleaming high-tech wheelchair, her mother at her side. The mother says, "Hi," and discreetly disappears downstairs. Mariana will call her when we are done. Having her mother in tow is not a luxury but is a simple necessity, since my patient is in rather advanced stages of multiple sclerosis (MS) and cannot get in and out of a cab on her own at this point. Really there are many things she cannot do now: she cannot work, cook, clean her apartment, walk her dog. Also she cannot dress herself, or bathe without help, or go to the bathroom. She is pretty and well groomed; her mother makes sure that she is clean, well fed, neatly dressed, like a well-kept child.

Mariana wheels herself in, settles at her usual spot, and smiles. Then she says, "Hi," and the syllable carries all the intimacy of a close friendship.

I like her; I have known her for a long time, long before the advance of her illness, since what seem now prehistoric times when she walked into my office complaining that she couldn't get over her unrequited love for a guy down the hall. She simply could not think about anything else, so she spent her days in bed fantasizing about him. School and work were out of question, she said. Of course it was much more than a case of a broken heart. It turned out that Mariana lived a strange half-charmed life. Since a very early age her job was to be her mother's confidant and companion, and she perfected her attunement to her mother's emotional states to an unbelievable degree of sensitivity. This skill, or sense of attunement, spilled into other areas of her life as well, and it was as if she had a sixth sense when it came to figuring out people. At the same time any practical thing, however small a step, presented an insurmountable difficulty, from which my patient usually escaped into her dreams, fantasies, memories, or simply sleep. Needless to say, her family situation, in spite of her mother's endless tirades of how Mariana should be more self-sufficient in everyday matters, supported the existing state of things.

It took us almost 4 years of slow meticulous work to bring Mariana back to reality. She finally got her first job and started thinking of going back to college.

It was then that Mariana realized that when she put her hand in her coat pocket, she could not tell by touch whether she had pennies or quarters there. That first sign of her sickness occurred about 5 years ago, and no member of the medical profession could stop the slow but steady decline going on ever since.

Today she is pensive. She takes her time before opening the verbal exchange. She says, "I think I am losing myself."

I am silent. She knows that I am there 100 percent, and I know that it's all she needs to continue exploration. And she does. "I mean all these people, you know, in the street, and those Mother brings to visit to keep me company. And on Pal talk [this is a chat room] too. I think at first they don't know what to do with me; I make them all very uncomfortable. And you know I try to make it OK, little jokes, and never calling things what they really are, the disgusting things, I mean. But they still are uncomfortable."

I find myself wondering about what's coming. I know that sick people like my patient, when they make themselves visible, tend to be unofficially placed into certain groups or categories, if you like, by the "not sick yet" members of the society, certain convenient group projections being at work—convenient in the sense that they allow others to deal with a set of well-defined fantasies, definitions, and rules, effectively erasing the word "person" from the notion of a "disabled person." This also implies a silent request that for the sake of acceptance the person herself should politely concur to vanish into "the disabled one." I wonder if Mariana with her sharpened attunement to others is also thinking about that. So she continues.

"But it doesn't matter. I wanted to say something else—you know I have this childhood friend, Liz. Always told me that I was fat, stupid, and lazy. Haven't seen her for years. So she called a week ago out of the blue, said that she talked to my mom, and learned that I was sick, and wanted to visit. And you know Liz comes, and looks at me like she never saw me before, with awe, I guess. And we start talking, and she actually listens to me, never happened before. And then right before she leaves, she says that it's amazing how misfortune changes a person, especially real sickness, how one gets wiser, and begins to realize the futilities of life. And I say, 'No, I think life is given for joy, and happiness.' And you know what, she ignored me, she said, 'Goodbye, I'll be back soon' as if I never said anything at all, like she never heard. And she is not stupid, you know. It's like she would want to put me in a box, sort of that I should say certain things, and I shouldn't say other things, and if I say them she just doesn't hear. And it's not just her, other people too. Like everybody thinks that I should be this or that, you know, usually 'a poor girl' and then they expect me to be super nice, and not to argue, and not to want sex, and never be angry, and some think that I am a nice stupid child sitting around while my mother takes care of me, and I swear some people feel that my MS can rub off on them."

There is a pause. Mariana looks out of the window, and I just let her be.

"You know," she starts again, "the worst thing is that I find myself becoming what they want, whoever it is, more now than before. I just catch myself afterward. Especially on Pal talk, easier, you know, when you are just a voice. Sort of drifting, you know. And so safe. Like I have my place. Makes everything so comfortable. And then I come here, and sort of wake up, because you know me, real me, and I get furious, and it feels like a return to myself. But then I drift again."

Well, it feels really good—her appreciation of me being able to put aside all of my preconceptions about sickness like hers and my discomfort seeing her in a wheelchair, and an occasional fantasy that she would call and cancel a session, so that I would not have to face the possibility of my own sickness, after all nobody ever knows, and the certainty of my own eventual death. I am proud of myself.

"Oh, by the way," Mariana flashes me one of those radiant smiles of hers, "I haven't made that appointment with the physiotherapist that we talked about last time. Lost his number. It's just been a difficult week. You know, one of those when I just want to sleep all the time. Mom promised to get it again and call him tomorrow. But actually I wanted to know what you think about Mozart. We had this great conversation yesterday, you know in my chat room again …"

I nod and find my thoughts drifting pleasantly to the subject of Mozart and how it is really good that being so disabled Mariana can think about other things and how it is so good that her mother takes really great care of her, like a mother should care for her sick child. Well, on the subject of Mozart … Wait a second—what was it? Child? Sick child? Where did that come from? The young woman in front of me is 28 years old and is certainly capable of making her own telephone calls. And then it dawns at me that I was proud of myself too soon, because a minute ago I slipped into a comfortable trap—a sick person as a well-kept child entertaining herself with nice toys, Mozart in our case. Well, in reality it was Mariana all over again, mortally afraid of any practical thing, drifting comfortably into the abstract intellectual world.

I look up, and she is waiting for what I am going to say about Mozart, eager and happy. I take a deep breath and say, "Well, what do you think stopped you from making that call?"

5

DORI

"O Thou Seer, Go, Flee Thee"*

EYAL ROZMARIN

EDITOR'S INTRODUCTION

It is important to see that we are as drawn to discourse as we feel imprisoned by it. One context for this book is the usual sort of writing on mind and politics in which society seems oppressive. But here we also understand discourse, including interpellation, as facilitative: Subjects of ourselves and subjects to social forces, we can have the social context we need only if we find ourselves through it. In relating his work with a patient, like him an Israeli immigrant, Eyal Rozmarin wants to connect the idea of discourse in critical theory to a newly reinterpreted notion of the collective unconscious. He reflects on how, separately and together, they relate to the Third of discourse in the room: how to live out their shared cultural mission to realize their potential for the nation and to realize themselves, an enterprise in which they may lose themselves as well.

Dori came into my office, a 29-year-old, strong-looking and handsome Israeli man—the kind they used to put on propaganda posters for national projects and the armed forces in Israel. He said this: "I have been living in New York for 5 years now. I have a nightclub that earns a lot of money. I can get any girl I want. I have good friends. I have the kind of life I thought I wanted. But I don't enjoy anything.

---

* Also Amaziah said unto Amos: "O thou seer, go, flee thee away into the land of Judah, and there eat bread, and prophesy there" (Amos 7:12).

אבנת משו, סחל מש-לכאו, הדוהי ץרא-לא ךל-חרב ךל הזח, סומע-לא היצמא רמאיו:

35

Most of the time I am bored and restless. I keep thinking, 'My life needs to be more than this.'

"So I decided to leave New York. This is my plan: I am going to find a deserted beach, somewhere on the Mediterranean, and found a place that would be something between a resort and a commune. I will live there. My friends will come to stay and work with me. There will be paying guests, but only people like us. It would be a place for resting and for thinking, a place where people come to learn how to be happy.

"It feels crazy to leave behind everything that I created, but it also feels right. And I know I can do it. I have the experience to put something like this together, and I have people that believe in me and would put money into anything I start. It is now January, I will be gone by April—I've given myself 3 months. But see, this is why I came to see you. I have a strange feeling that this plan is not completely mine. It was my idea. I still think this is what I need to do to give my life meaning. But it also feels like the idea was put into my mind. Like it is what I want but also not what I want. Like I am going to change my life completely without knowing why. I need to understand this feeling before I do it. There is too much doubt."

It may be surprising, but nothing in what Dori said seemed strange to me. On the contrary—sitting with him in my New York office, everything he said made sense. I was immediately swept into his story. It felt intensely relevant to me. If anything was strange, it was how quickly and how much Dori's dilemma seemed familiar. In an instant there was between us something brotherly.

These feelings that I had are, I believe, worth mentioning, because they reflected something very powerful that happened between us—a sort of kinship that transpired and made it possible for us to see and go where we could not have otherwise. There is the obvious: We are both of the same place and roughly the same time. We share a world of references and experiences, from what the beach feels like on a summer afternoon to names of secret army units. But there is more: There is within and underneath the obvious a vast collective story in which we both partake, and that played through and between us from the start. This shared story, in which the Israeli beach and Israeli army are recent characters, enabled us to feel and recognize each other in a world common to the two of us.

Yet what happened between Dori and me is an extreme case of what happens and what we hope will happen in any meaningful encounter, including that of the analytic kind. It is what we still tend to admit in psychoanalysis only apologetically as subjective fantasies called transference and countertransference. But what we should perhaps reconsider as the shared foundations of our lives.

Back to the story: If there was a sense of familiarity, it was familiarity in a time of crisis. Dori's dilemma needed urgent figuring out. There was a plan, and there was something strange and unidentifiable about it. So much so that he could not begin to realize it. That made me ask: If this is not your plan, whose plan is it? Dori took a moment.

As I waited, my question started multiplying in my mind: Why should you leave behind everything that you've created? Why should you go into the desert without knowing where or how? Who is chasing you out of your present? Who is luring you with the idea of a utopia, making you think that leaving is the only way to redeem your life? It is not as if you are a slave and this is Egypt. It is not as if you are a Jew and this is Germany, when our grandparents were young. Who says that you must flee or you will perish? Why does all of this sound like a calling?

As he kept silent and I thinking, Dori's plan began to seem to me like a personal variation on a major theme in Jewish history. It is a theme originating in Abraham's near sacrifice of his son as proof of unquestioned loyalty; a theme played in the story of Israel's exodus from Egypt, and the sentencing to death of an entire generation, for doubting, and thus betraying, the prophecy of a return to the promised land; a theme repeated most recently in the form of Zionism. There is a call, echoing both cruel necessity and transcendental promise, a command inspiring with the idea of duty and seducing with the possibility of free will. And underneath it all a founding paradox that runs through our history until this day, decreeing, that for the sake of the collective, its sons must return from a foreign present to a future home and in so doing may be lost.

How could Dori's dilemma have not made sense to me? We were both born into this epic narrative. We are both sons of a collective that has not only dreamt but has also acted on its dreams under the ethos of being cursed in being chosen. A collective that was apocalyptically reduced to ashes in the generation of our grandparents, only to regain itself in power—billed as miracle—in the hands of our parents, their children. We were both raised under the contradiction that a good life consists of normalcy—achievable only through extraordinary efforts. And each of us once already felt it necessary to realize a dream of personal utopia—in transition, having moved from Israel to New York, where we now meet. Now here he is, talking with me about a present that did not keep its promise, thinking up a new future that this time feels as suspicious as it is obligatory. No wonder Dori's story made sense to me. But how can we talk about it in psychoanalysis?

We are all talking here about the not-given in the distinction between the social and the individual, between what, from another angle, feels to the self as inside or outside. In this we are trying to address a wide gap between ideas formed in the structuralist and post-structuralist traditions about how social discourse founds subjectivity and the typical psychoanalytic focus on individuals in their immediate environments. We all agree that social discourse both limits and enables the possibilities of the subject. But there has been a shift in our allegiance over time. If conforming, or adapting—as old ego psychology would call it—was once seen as the ultimate achievement, we are now more focused on how living within the normative can be oppressive and depressing to the individual. Yet both of these positions share a basic premise: Taking part in the collective story—although it may be necessary—is a melancholic compromise. What I would like to highlight is another angle: There is inherent to the dialectic between the subject and the many discourses in which he is founded, not only confinement in subjection but also meaningful belonging and participating, which are the conditions of everything intersubjective.

If there is a basic notion in psychoanalysis, it is that of an unconscious—a register outside subjective consciousness that all the same has great effect on how the subject thinks and feels and how he lives his life. If there is any promise in psychoanalysis, it is in our expanding our attention from the alleged inside of the subject, to what happens between subjects, that is, to the relational. Putting the old notion of the unconscious into this new framework already made possible the idea of a relational unconscious. It also made possible the notion of the Third—which is, in my mind, a specific kind of relational unconscious formed within a dyad. We now recognize in psychoanalysis the great effect of all kinds of collective discourse on the subject and are already—in the Third—contemplating a notion of an unconscious that is not within subjects but between them. There is no reason, then, not to think an unconscious born before and common to—more than the two of the analytic dyad—an unconscious shared among the members of any group drawn in a social or historical discourse. We may, in other words, want to consider a more current version of an old psychoanalytic notion, of an unconscious formed, inherited, and shared in a collective.

I believe that the familiarity I sensed with Dori and learned later that he felt together with me had to do with the two of us sharing an unconscious: a grand historical third born when god gave Isaac back to Abraham in return for marking him in circumcision—and still going. It was not only that we have similar personal histories and so we understood each other. It was also that both of our lives are manifestations of a complex collective fantasy. We are both Jewish Israeli men of a certain generation. We became subjects through and against a specific chapter in a collective narrative with its dreams and conflicts. Our subjective dilemmas, how we feel confined and where we see promise—the entire grid of meaning onto which we plot our subjective experience—is anchored in this collective discourse. And so we could not but have had between us our collective—unconscious, defying any simple definition of self-boundaries.

I use the terms *collective narrative, discourse*, and *unconscious* interchangeably, to the degree that they, in a sense, all point to the same—that which is common and definitive of subjects who are members in collectives but is all the same not marked and present as (a conscious experience) of the subject. Dori and I belong in a particularly extreme collective, extreme not only since it has been so long pushed together but also since it puts such a deliberate effort into maintaining self consciousness of its collectivity. Yet we all share commonalities with others: from the national and ethnic, through gender and sexuality, to more particular ways we are marked and take our place in the social. We are all quick to sense and look for those commonalties when we meet a stranger. We do it in psychoanalysis, too. Only what we look for is what's privileged in our collective discourse—we look for certain types of so-called universals. My experience with Dori taught me how powerfully we live and must therefore recognize the particular collective forces that act in and within us.

Some people live with relative ease in the junction of discourses where their subjectivities transpire. Others feel dis-ease. Dori came en route to once again being driven up the ramp onto the collective highway. But he had a strong if unclear sense that his travel plans where the effect of something other than himself. He stayed in New York a while longer. We encountered more of that other in his subjectivity in the form of deep, if tormented, responsibility and loyalty to significant others, and the collective stories their lives realized. As they surfaced, Dori became increasingly aware of how forcefully these collective stories identified him. It was difficult, but it made it possible for him to have some sense of freedom and to be able to deliberate how he wanted to partake in these stories and where he wanted to draw boundaries, which is perhaps the most that is possible for any of us.

6

EDE

Race, the Law, and I

ORNA GURALNIK

EDITOR'S INTRODUCTION

In the context of the United States, interpellation is perhaps most visible, even tangible, in the arena of race and racism. Orna Guralnik tells us of Ede, a Nigerian immigrant suffering from depersonalization and struggling to be interpellated out of her postcolonial Blackness. This struggle manifests in the treatment relationship, as Guralnik, experiencing her Whiteness, tracks their mutual run-in with racial interpellation at the nexus of class, ethnicity, money, and public power.

At my door is beautiful Ede. Surprise: She is Black. Laura never mentioned that in her referral, nor did I twig when Ede phoned. Within minutes, I am dazzled by her intelligence and poetry, postmodern talk, and street humor.

Ede hasn't really been here for the past 20 of her 27 years: "A part of me was left on that airplane from Nigeria." She is perpetually depersonalized, sleep-deprived, slightly psychotic: "I know this sounds crazy, but my plants terrify me, they seem hungry, human, they want something from me ... did I feed them a fertilizer that made them this way ...?"

Ede eyes me. My Axis I sirens rattling, I maintain my posture: staring back at her, I feel her steadying too. She is writing a novel about "a person who killed themselves and came back, looking for when they felt happy." Melancholy. What has she lost? After many college writing awards, she fears what is emerging in her novel. She thinks race had a lot to do with both the awards she had received and with her writer's block now.

"I am angrier than other Blacks"—Ede scans me, assessing my race sensibilities. I am speechless; competing discourses vie for my interpretive executive center. I seek my location, a White person trying to grasp something of being an Other.

In our culture, hooks (1995) contends, people of color quash a killing rage as daily discrimination piles up unacknowledged. Blacks who progress and gain economic proximity with Whites often buy into liberal individualism, which de-links personal from collective fate: "By demanding that black people … annihilate our rage in order to assimilate … white folks urge us to remain complicit with their efforts to colonize, oppress, and exploit" (p. 16). This de-linking of individuals from their sociopolitical context impoverishes the mind (Layton, 2006b). It activates dissociative dynamics (Guralnik, 2007); melancholically foreclosed into the world of the abject, individuals lose their ability to feel fully present and personified.

She feels comfortable with me, Ede declares, sweeping us into hopefulness. As she leaves, I send her off with Leonard Pitt's (2004) essay "Crazy Sometimes," where he describes the daily assaults of racism denied while happening. Marking our first base: Ede and I; Us against the State and the world's racists; most comfortable location to conduct psychoanalysis. She leaves, and I am skeptical: But how long can we stay here? Of White people's kindness, Toni Morrison (1992) says they have to pity a thing before they could like it …

My second surprise: Ede talks White. With her family, her Nigerian accent booms deep, her sentences short and metaphoric. In public, she passes as African American, hip, predatory. With White folks, she works another game, appeasing with reasonableness. I am uneasily grateful for her "White-girl" talk. My own "Whiteness" (a recently earned privilege for a Jew) is an "unthought known" for me. What's in skin color? Only later do I read of Fanon's (1967) postcolonial, inferiority-struck Negro, whose inferiority issues from a doubling: Over economic inferiority lies "the internalization, or better, the epidermalization" (pp. 10–11) of that inferiority.

Ede is caught in the postcolonial wish: to be interpellated out of her originary blackness. From her Western perch, she sees scum and humiliation in her family, their home filthy, dilapidated. Responding to this shameful heritage, she got into the strange habit of ordering entire gardens—flower plants, trees, and landscaping instructions—over the Internet to be shipped to her mother, in the hope of beautifying her history retroactively. Sensing this historical pull, her mother e-mails, "I know you were raised in this country; still, it does not relieve you of your skin. We are what make you who you are, whether you think we are good or bad…. The X after running from himself all his life goes down as an X. There is no choice."

Ede seeks legitimation, class restoration. Her mother was a bastard to a Nigerian princess. Her once upper-middle-class father became involved, once in the United States, in endless pyramid schemes (his own father was a policeman for the Brits during colonial times). Ede's is a personal, transgenerational, and political quest for race and class mobility.

I study Nigeria's reputation as premier international exporter of 419 schemes. A World Bank study (The World Bank, 2010) describes Nigeria, so rich in resources (coco, rubber), as mired in a culture of rent seeking and corruption created by "easy" oil. Rather than becoming a sub-Saharan empire through taxable wealth, its economy keeps stalling and society destabilizes. I note the striking parallel between Nigeria's stagnation and Ede's trajectory. Yet in this insight I forget to know my Whiteness, fount of trauma from slave trades to current Western global trade: *We* pump oil out and corruption in.

Regulatory discourse enters us in various ways, including our legal system and what it legitimizes and abjects. We—White middle class—typically deem the law guarantor of safety and fairness. Yet we forget that one of its functions is the uneven allocation of social power and resources among groups. By decreeing what will be criminal and what permissible (MacKinnon, 2005), the law shapes access to human dignity, resources, physical security, credibility, and power. Particularly in the United States, legal discourse naturalizes racial divisions. And indeed, Ede was confused: Did her skin color earn her legal protection—class action, access to funding? Or increased risk of being targeted by local police?

***

We settle into a steady work rhythm. Ede's depressive, psychotic-like symptoms recede. More palpable rage surfaces. Daily living infuriates: harassed in her poor neighborhood, stared down by Black neighbors for dating an Asian, envying White girlfriends enjoying an ease that she could never imagine feeling entitled to.

One day Ede arrived in turmoil and bewilderment:

Ede: I was fired, Orna ... I don't know what I'm gonna do.
Me: Oh, no—what happened??
Ede: He singled me out! Of course, I am the only woman, no, the only black woman, he found his scapegoat once and for all. I'm not even sure what happened, but he fired me on the spot.

Ede read being fired as a sign of racism. I worried: She needed work's structure, not activism's whirl. In her first version, she was fired for having tried to organize all the employees to clarify their work systems and priorities. Yet it soon became clear that, in the general meeting she called while her boss was on vacation, she had revealed secret financial figures and processes that denied employees better benefits (401Ks and vacations), access to which she had as her boss's right hand. The cause of her immediate firing—"inciting unrest"—did not compute for her: She bore shame through gender and race.

Me: What were you imagining your boss would think of this meeting when he came back?
Ede: I thought the pressure would make him understand that he can't just go on treating people like this.

Ede's naïveté about rules of conduct shocked me. I found myself doing psycho-socio-ed: If you deceive your boss to provoke dissent, you should expect to be fired. Ede's outrage was registering with me as her clinging to victimhood while refusing to own her personal power and responsibility. Isn't de-linking personal responsibility from collective destiny what Clarence Thomas, the conservative African-American United States Supreme Court Justice, promotes? What a strange place to find myself. When your "medical gaze" unites with hegemonic powers, a kind of sanctimony underscores your interpretations.

Things deteriorated. Ede consulted two attorneys: They were promising $3 million in damages from a discrimination suit! No, she did
not intend to seek another job, and actually, if she was about to land
a lot of money, school did not seem urgent either. One lawyer sent
her, wired with recording devices, to maneuver a conversation with
her ex-boss so he would sound racist and sexist. She was developing mesmerizing omnipotence, a superhero destined to bring down
the system. And me? In response to her disapproval I indeed started
wondering: Had I neglected to notice the endless discrimination
she suffered while working for this man? Was I colluding with the
social order by not being more outraged on a daily basis? Missing my
empathic analytic compass, I was worried but still judgmental of both
her loss of interest in becoming a good, self-supporting citizen and
the evaporation of her artistic passions. Her leaning on the system
for unemployment and potential legal extraction of enormous sums
of money seemed disastrous and plain wrong. Something about her
unambivalent sense of entitlement to unearned compensation was disturbing my sensibilities.

But I finally could feel my color, my Whiteness. Race stood between
us, our skin interpellating us into different legal orders. Legal forces
structure how one is allowed to think about the interrelated social
categories of race, gender, and class. I believe events follow certain
lawfulness: Citizens have a fair contract with their governing authorities. Indeed, psychoanalytic practice rests entirely on Judeo-Christian
assumptions: "You work hard, you succeed; you do something wrong,
you get punished." But is this part of the privilege of living in the
first world? For it is also an ideology, applying only to a certain class,
to mask its partiality and to minimize resistance to prevailing power
structures. It holds only as long as we are not suddenly in a "state of
emergency." But I was in a "state of exception" (Agamben, 2005) — I
wanted Ede compliant.

But Ede's world is a back-breaking reality of inescapable poverty,
where being a good citizen has nothing to do with being treated
right. When you lack the ability to influence one way, you try others—you steal and redistribute, create a mess for the heck of it, or
try your own risky mutiny. Still, a hidden sense of justice lurks: You

expect the world to set history right and compensate you for what went so very wrong.

Ede had a perverse relationship to the law; she stole from privileged college girlfriends, spent the petty cash of a workplace where she felt mistreated. She was bothered by these transgressions, but it was not remorse. Intoxicating, they also left her dysregulated with no reliable internal structure. What seemed a moral lacuna expressed her powerlessness, an attempt to set things right. I took inspiration from Robin Hood rather than Melanie Klein (1964).

Lawlessness typified Ede's family history. Men in her family were free to molest her, to which she would respond by entering a near-sleep state as if in a duty-free zone between legal systems. She and her brothers were punched, forced to "pick the pin" on their knees, beaten with a stick if they didn't recite the times tables. Her mind doubled; colonization seemed the right response to a bad body.

**

I rescheduled a session. Ede showed up on a Saturday, finding an empty suite: "Just me and the cleaning woman"—she spat, her eyes launching a class action suit against my practice of hiring cleaning ladies of color.

Saturday? I don't work weekends. She was adamant, disgusted by my haughty certainty that the error was hers. She warned me not to even think of charging her for this missed session and while at it questioned the ethics of my entire pay-for-missed-session policy. Next, after accruing a debt on her already reduced fee, Ede questioned my bill: "I don't believe I did not pay you for October!" She berated my antiquated billing system.

Our implicit therapeutic contract was unraveling. Ede, dreamlike: "Hmmm, funny, I've been looking at your September bill, and I don't have anything written down for those extra sessions you marked here. Don't you think that's strange?" Me, driven more than a little crazy: "You are pulling the rug from under every stable point of reality! How do you expect me to respond? Forego payment?" Ede, confused about what she really expected my reaction to be: "I guess not; that wouldn't make sense."

Basic lawfulness, the rug being pulled from under us, originates, in Benjamin's (2004) view, between mother and infant. Contra Lacan's idea of the Law of the Father—the Third—Benjamin finds preliminary Thirdness in the synchronous, matching patterns of interaction between infant and mother that are joyfully negotiated by way of affective responsiveness, freely, not by submission. Instead of a Lacanian mental representation through speech, Benjamin proposes an Energic Third that allows a Moral Third, itself permitting the representation of different perspectives and averting the kill-or-be-killed positions, while the Paternal Third in mother's mind prevents merger with her child.

Ede and I were missing this underlying basis. We were searching: How does a Nigerian and Jewish dyad find synchrony here, recreate a mini-universe in which laws prevail? How about: We both show up for appointments. On time. Unresentfully, I charge her according to her means. She pays, on time. If she accuses me of lying, she should expect some outrage from me. If I am messy with my billing, I should expect her to be rattled and question me. She is not sure she can live in our universe, but she is giving it a chance. And I am not sure this mini-universe bears on her real world, other than offering her an island from which she may be able to wage more powerful acts of mutiny.

As for the lost Saturday session, we create a neutral zone wherein no reality prevails. I clip her $100 bill to her chart but do not deposit it. Out of her account but not in mine: It is our borrowed universe. It sits between us every session, waiting for us to find some legitimate truth—who does this money belong to? She influences the rules of the game: I change my record-keeping system.

We begin construing her psychotic-like experiences as her portal to lost beauty—African gods, magic, trance-inducing drumming and music, colors, her large, warm family, the farmlands. In the thick of this work, Ede fell into a short phase of intense reverie, bordering on hallucinations. She lay in a trance for 2 days, alternating between what she located as womb experiences and early memories of her nanny being exorcised. She was seeking transcendence, a "new goddess," an alternative universe where she is not always already stamped by history, rebirth.

She revisited this topic of lawfulness in a new way. Full frontal, she was speaking to the mother of all hegemonies: "You have treated me as sub-human for generations…. You colonized me, you treated me like a piece of garbage, the men continued to rape me and deny me, and my mother had no voice from which to say Stop! ... I do not exist for you! Yet you want me to obey your rules and regulations?! I know nothing of your idea of responsibility ..."

During this otherworldly session, tears roll as we fiercely talk about living among so many injustices and trying to maintain small islands of genuine mutual respect. I want that for us, but I am also implicated in what stands between us and is not fixable in our world. My Nigerian patient confronts me with Whiteness, its license, guilt, and shame. Her injustices revealing my privilege. Shielded by the Law.

FACING REALITY TOGETHER

Discussion of "The Social Third"

JESSICA BENJAMIN

The aim of this fascinating and successful collection of diverse clinical writings is to open up the space wherein individual psyches and psychoanalytic dyads are infused and delimited by discursive systems. More than a shifting series of stage sets, the discursive practices that are illuminated in these chapters are parts of selves, as crucial to the interactions as any other part-selves that engage in the analytic dyad. We now see how so much that appears to happen against the backdrop of this "social third" (Altman, 2009, p. 61) is actually constructed by its shapes and shadows—that even if we are able to see around and beyond it, we cannot undo its powerful staging effects because they are the very stuff of which our meanings and intentions are made.

At times this exposure of effects is stunning, at other moments more a confirmation of what was suspected or familiar, but in every case beyond what we could have discerned and articulated minus the supposition that, as Eyal Rozmarin (Chapter 5) eloquently puts it, "the entire grid of meaning onto which we plot our subjective experience is anchored in … collective discourse." This supposition, this awareness, changes what we are able to see and how we strive to imagine what we cannot see or glimpse only darkly.

These chapters are so rich. Deciding where to insert my own thoughts and questions amid this array of possible stories and analyses is daunting. The choice may itself be revealing, but since I must begin somewhere, I shall. Each of these chapters, condensed as it may be, deserves a discussion of its own, but I am going to have to sacrifice some of the particularity to the general and highlight some themes. I believe it's my mission here, which I have chosen to accept, to highlight what is gained or lost or made more troublesome by admitting

49

the intensity of interpellation our psychoanalyst authors allow themselves to experience.

What Are Mommies (Little Girls) Made of?

I'm going to start with the "mommy stuff," precisely because it is
familiar, endlessly discussed, yet in some way elusive for each mother
and each analytic couple who pursue its outlines in the fog. I want to
suggest that the interpellation described by Maura Sheehy (Chapter
1) confronts us with a dilemma that is insoluble in its own terms. But
this insolubility could plausibly be seen in two ways: either in terms of
the interminable psychoanalytic dilemma of being (or having) a "bad
mother," or in terms of the adage, "a woman's work is never done."
Never being good enough could be linked to a profound sense that
in our unsafe society children can never be protected or given enough
to make them safe, as Lazarre (1991) described in *Worlds Beyond My
Control*. But why should mothers, or anyone, be able to guarantee this
safety to children in a life in which we are all subject to a variety of
slings and arrows? We suspect that the heightened expectations of
provision may enter our minds more by channeling our baby selves,
baby fears, and desires (e.g., unconscious fears of environmental failure, annihilation, abandonment), than merely by dint of social infla-
tion and competition. Yet the confusion of good enough mothering
with the ability to protect children and give them a perfect life ("his
majesty the baby," as Freud [1914] already delineated in the discussion of narcissism) seems indeed a cultural discourse, an artifact of
what Lasch (1979) dubbed the "culture of narcissism." The direction
of effects is doubled: discourses into which we are interpellated have,
as psychoanalysts insist, origins in specific infantile or childhood
fantasies.

Thus, the question of the nature of Melissa's badness as a mother,
and her analyst's badness or inadequacy, remains open. The question
is not why women as mothers can't get a grip but why they think
they should have one—and such an omnipotent and perfect one at
that? Which baby is calling that shot, and what anxiety dictates that
mother should keep her Cheerios in the bag and be as efficient and
buttoned up as Mary Poppins? Or, put differently, what is inside the

bag? What logic of demand was previously obscured by its cover, by that foggy feeling of "not good enough" mother or analyst? Beneath or besides this guilty sense of lack, what other discourses are lurking? Behind the perfect mommy imperative, for instance, is there a powerful discourse of gender? One in which perfect little girls never feel good enough, have to be more and more perfect in their bodies, their behavior, their scholarship, their skills in the girl group, and so on?

In psychoanalytic terms, these discourses are collective curative fantasies, elaborated by each individual, of redeeming herself or others by being perfectly maternal and giving, or perfectly accomplished and balanced. The redemptive fantasy of the omnipotent mother who can be all-giving is one I've (Benjamin, 1994) considered in depth because it seemed to me so prevalent when I was in Maura's situation. Maura herself has to recognize how, still hostage to this fantasy, she has to give it up to help her patient. This is a lovely example of the theme common to many in this group of relational narrations: that the analyst's self-recognition is so essential because the analyst is struggling with the same thing as the patient. And therefore her breakthrough—at times shared dramatically as in this case—is essential to the patient's. This is a point that time and again has been made in relational writing about enactment: Patient and analyst are implicated in the enactment through a shared (unconscious) fantasy. But as Maura's vignette illustrates, this point is more subtle than might at first glance appear. The act of disclosure—as in, oh yes, I'm messy, as Cheerios reveal the not-so-cheery side of juggling career and motherhood—is more than a revelation to dispel the illusion of perfection.

It changes the terms of psychoanalysis because it is more than a disclosure; it is an invitation to face reality together, a most powerful instantiation of surrendering to the third, to "life as it really is, not as we wish it to be." To negate our simple subjection to the shared fantasy—with the challenge, Who says it's easy for me?—involves enlisting our patient as an analytic subject who can engage the "secret" truth together; it is calling upon the space of intersubjectivity to share a third that is in fact not unconscious. Rather, this third is a deliberately created alternative to our unconscious submersion in the unquestioned realm of the ideal. This third dissolves the idealization of what could or should have been, including that of an analyst who should or could be the "real thing"—the thing that is never reality. A different kind of ideal object, one that might be lovable in its imperfect reality, survives. Fantasy that persecutes with its redemptive demand gives way to a piece of more authentic conversation; that moment of interaction, a piece of enacted play, begins to create an intersubjective space as an alternative to unquestioned unconscious submission and fantasy substitutes.

It strikes me as incredibly apt that Maura is talking about reclaiming the subjectivity and desire not only outside of the house (not just when she puts on makeup and goes to the office) but also in motherhood. There is thus a parallel between the mother's longing for intimate closeness with her child (wanting to get inside each other's minds, share secrets) and between analyst and patient. How much can we recognize, own, make use of our analytic desire to have an intimate relationship with our patients, based on knowing and being known? Because, after all, we indeed share such vital raw aspects of the human condition together even when we don't expose them so concretely by spilling the details of our version.

Down in the Dumps of Good Gayness

Interestingly, the dyad Stephen Hartman (Chapter 2) describes with Darren seems to me the example most closely allied to Maura's experience of looking for goodness. This linkage appears doubly, in the frustrated desires for intimacy as a mutually constructed issue in the treatment and in the obstacle to that intimacy posed by redemptive fantasies of perfection or having it all. Stephen's conclusion that brings the two, analyst and patient, up against the wall of shattered hopes for overcoming one's "othered" identity is that we can't be good boys, either in hetero or homo sense, in either alternative or straight discourses of goodness. We can be neither ideally wildly "bad" nor fit for normative *New York Times* good-boy-hood. Stephen's paper lights up the shadows of gender as melancholy, a position of denying one's love that Butler (1995) so powerfully articulated: the search for love denied that takes the form of hating what one really is, longing for what one can never have or be. In Darren's history, not being able to light up his father, lacking the longed-for connection of homo-erotic identificatory love, has led to a rather confused form of ideal love. Here I refer to the idea (Benjamin, 1988, 1995) that, absent a parental mirror, response to the excitement and love in such iden-tification leads a child to confuse the yearning for the denied love with submission. More specifically, the confusion in his redemptive fantasy was amplified by the contradiction in the primary parental couple he grew up with. Is the marital bliss Darren fails to achieve constituted by being what his mother was to his father? (A further confusion given that he can't decide if father was the man hiding out in the basement or the one banging his mother on the party wall?) Or does bliss lie in being its opposite, an exhibitionistic gay hero who is only protected by, but not deadened and reduced to, the patina of a normalized partnership?

Like perfect motherhood lost in confusion, perfect partnership relates to a cultural narrative that can make Stephen feel as undone as Darren—"We're both fucked!" But there's an added dimension of explicit envy and desire in this story that complicates the moment of sharing the third, the realization of what it means to be a gay man subject to the laws of a homophobic society. Stephen represents not only what Darren feels he can never be but also what he can never have. Yet, in my take on the erotic transference, Darren needs a chance to feel he can both be and have Stephen just enough—enough to love himself rather than hating himself compared with the ideal self he projects outward. Is the question how will he, or can he, get enough identificatory love from Stephen to make up for what he didn't get from his father? Or is it how will he move from melancholy to mourning what he didn't get? As long as Darren believes Stephen has "It" and envies it, he can't mourn. So what must Stephen do or be to address Darren's desire? Perhaps something crucial is (unavoidably?) elided when Stephen shifts voice in his narration from Darren's wish to surrender to a more abstract statement of his limit: "Imagine being able to tolerate binding the most degenerate sex with the surest love? Darren can't. We haven't. I am, for Darren, married, and he is, for me, a patient." Are those the obstacles?

I find myself wondering. What causes the analyst to back off here; what really underlies the failure of imagination? Surely plenty of analysts and patients have imagined being married, but imagining the surest love coupled with most degenerate sex—is that excessive, too hot to handle, what the discourse in fact won't allow or contain? Or is it too confusing to couple submissive accommodation (you can do what you will with me) with secure attachment? At the very least the failure to imagine combining attachment and sexual heat is key: Perhaps the height of sexual melancholy for straight and gay is that the discursive practice of monogamy and marriage simply doesn't hold or create space for the transgressive aspects of sex; it can't take the heat. Is this lack of a social container for desire the reason that the analyst is left simply too alone trying to handle it by himself, while handling it with the patient is too hot? Perhaps Stephen's example pushes us to recognize the point at which a shared third joined around resistance to a regulatory discourse in which one's desire is delegitimated—sighing over the *Times*—is just so much easier to bear than the third that joins us in that desire. In other words, desire may frighten us simply with its otherness: The dyad is challenged at the point of restrained and contained revelation of dissociated yearnings for the surrender of love mingled with the vulnerability of innocence and transgression.

Facing the Unspeakable Losses

On the other side, sometimes even the freedom to resist normativity appears foreclosed. Resistance to what traps us in acceptance of our socially defined abjection as other, the dehumanized identity of other to the same, is not so easy to muster, as Olga Pugachevsky (Chapter 4) discovers. The actual dehumanization of illness, the determining reality of her patient's loss of agency, its crippling function, can appear simply objective. As such it would seem to override the domain of subjective freedom and thus lull or overwhelm the analyst into submission. The dangerous thread of passivity in abjection that can be erotized by Darren is no less seductive, if perhaps more lethal, for Mariana. Her illness appears as the manifestation of lost agency and not merely its cause, and this appearance threatens Olga with a guilty sense of blaming the victim. She finds herself marshalling her mental forces to pierce the fog of illness, but the enactment that might invite Mariana to know her struggle, which could be seen as a struggle between different part selves has not yet manifested. Olga must side-step the temptation to collude in Mariana's stigmatization and lack of agency but must do so from the uncomfortable position of being part of the healthy world that is spared such abjection. The reality seems bleak: In addressing the phone call she cannot simply be the other to the part of Mariana's self that wishes to avoid, deny, escape her condition. She must address the condition in which the self that wants to live is really at the brink of facing a terrible helplessness to fulfill that wish, ever, in this life. Yet the self that can live, the one that wants to give in to passivity and be saved from outside, suffers equally, feeling victimized, ashamed, and resentful.

This is an overwhelming dilemma, in the face of which Olga must summon all her strength. The analyst's dissociated self-state parallels the patient's, necessitating a reflection on the intersubjective "we" who have failed to deal with her fear of action. Unlike Stephen's "we" who haven't dealt with the desire for surrender or the wish for normalcy, this dyad must tread more carefully at the edge of mourning, facing the fear of collapse and death. The ideal has not been named; the desire to live is itself, perhaps, too dangerous to even spin a fantasy that could be relinquished. In this constellation the analyst is simply struggling for life, for a place in her mind that can face how dissociated we become in the hopelessness of a loss that is dehumanizing not only because of its discursive aspects. What would it mean to face this trauma of losing a body that works in the world as well as the lack of agency it induces? Yet in this struggle Olga has to free herself from something within, a revulsion or fear of identification that is generated not only by illness per se but a cultural discourse in which vulnerability is abjected. The therapist is alone with her patient, abandoned by any social third, facing the patient's inevitable enmeshment with her mother as socially, not just psychically, constituted. To come to any truthful action requires consciousness of the burden she carries because the social world leaves her alone with Mariana: another aspect of the victimhood that such a social world generates. Olga and Mariana share this unspoken abandonment, in the face of which Olga, too, struggles to find voice and agency.

Sharing Our Stories: The Therapist's Use of Her Own Trauma

Our patients give us very different ways of facing trauma with them, of allowing us to enter their world, depending in part on their own sense of what repair will actually mean. By contrast to Mariana, Li-an (Chapter 3) seems to have a steadfast belief in her own agency, which never falters. For all the burden of badness and responsibility that was heaped upon her, she was expected to take an active role in dealing with disaster. This demand for action in the face of traumatic loss of homeland and social belonging as well as her parents de-idealization and harshness played a large role in Li-an's development. Interestingly, the need for agency in the face of trauma was consistently undertheo-rized, even scotomized by the early psychoanalytic discourse despite obvious experiences documented by those such as Anna Freud (Freud & Burlingham, 1943) during World War II. The helplessness of those original hysteria patients who succumbed to the demand for passiv-ity and inaction, such as Freud described, contrasts sharply with the efforts at restorative action taken (but not supported) by both Dora and Anna O. As I've described elsewhere (Benjamin, 1998), Anna O, Freud's pseudonym for Bertha Pappenheim, pulled herself together by becoming a feminist activist on behalf of women captive in sexual slavery or impoverished and outcast.

Unlike Pappenheim, Li-an encounters an analyst willing to look at herself and support Li-an's activities on her behalf. Her activity, her self-reflective narration of her story, drives the treatment forward and eventuates in a conflict Glenys Lobban must solve not only by recog-nizing cultural difference but also by encountering her own past. In a way, this is the most dramatic encounter of the analyst with herself that a patient can bring about—a reversal that earlier analysts were not capable of, as they shunned their own traumatic war experiences and objectified the patient.

The conflict between Li-an and Glenys adds a new twist to what I've said so far about fantasies and idealizations that are so often shared, discursive phenomena, which function like objects of melancholic attachment. Generally, the analysis of these objects, when it becomes part of an intersubjective process of affectively meaningful communication including mourning or pleasure in self-discovery, is part of what we think of as healing. But it does not exclude conflict, nor do we necessarily have the same idea as our patients about how such reparative fantasies should be re- or dissolved. Li-an doesn't want to give hers up, and Glenys is the one transformed in this story by Li-an's insistence.

Is this primarily a matter of decentering from one's own cultural context in which such social reparation would seem a mere dream? Or is there, as Glenys asks at the end, another read possible? What struck me on first hearing this story was how Li-an's desire to repair her parents paralleled the therapeutic endeavor that brings us to try to heal our patients (how many times have I heard supervisees slip and call them parents?). In this sense the cultural and individual level are not so distinct: Glenys not only hails from and was hailed into a less reconciling culture and a historical time when the trauma of being a soldier was occluded, but she also has a specific experience of failure that finally surfaces: Her hope that she could heal her wounded Dad on the fateful trip to England was dashed. In other words, did she fear reliving the disappointment and pain that was dissociated on that trip through Li-an's story? Had it occurred earlier, would such a recollection of her lost experience have changed her ability to hope for Li-an to succeed rather than anxious need to protect her from a similar fate? I am struck by the fact that similarity, rather than difference, joins Glenys and Li-an across culture: the wish to repair their parents. This common longing links therapists and patients, perhaps more deeply than we can often be aware. Li-an's striving to face and repair her parents' losses liberates Glenys to know her own losses and perhaps to mourn her father's in a very different way than before. The limitation Glenys faced is not simply cultural differences in attachment to one's family and tribe; it is also the old psychoanalytic discourse according to which the therapist is not meant to intrude with her own story. Thus she less quickly brings to bear her own story, but when she does it becomes apparent just how enriching it is to the therapeutic dyad.

How Well We Know Each Other: Therapist and
Patient in the Grip of the Same History

Eyal Rozmarin's patient (Chapter 5) confronts him head-on with the
narrative of exile, redemption, and exile that is common to more than
one generation of Israeli, but his story leaves me in suspense. I am
waiting not for the arrival in the promised land—fortunately, we are
told, the patient has given up creating his new utopian community for
the now—but awaiting the moment when the loss of that promise is
known in a new way. What will Eyal, his patient, and I, too, do when
we truly know that it is gone, lost, sacrificed to the very desire that
gave birth to it? As I know from my own history, revolutions devour
their own children, and the sons who are sacrificed to maintain the
promised land leave it not merely to save themselves but because
something terrible and unnamed has occurred.

The appeal of an epic, apocalyptic narrative is splendidly evoked by
Eyal's narration of his shared story. As Muriel notes, we are as much
drawn to discourse as we are driven, we are facilitated in the emergence of our subjectivity and not merely oppressed. In other words,
discourse does not merely interpellate by force, it compels, seduces,
fascinates, and then perhaps betrays us. Indeed, Eyal's vignette makes
vivid what I have already said (Benjamin, 1994) about redemptive
fantasies regarding eros or motherhood—but with the difference that
this fantasy is explicitly collective, and that is part of the salvation it
promises and fascination it holds. There are so many known elements:
The idea of returning to a home, creating a home, sacrificing what you
already have, saving a chosen few.

Analyst and patient are swimming in the same sea, literally and
figuratively. They are in it up to their necks. "Life needs to be more,"
says Dori, by which he means that life without that collective narrative loses a meaning, an intensity, a purpose that he was raised to
need and fulfill. To regard the process of taking part in the collective
as a melancholic compromise, Eyal shows us, may be too simple. It
does not take account of the need to belong, to be part of a collective story, to own our shared unconscious in a consciously relational
and collective way. What Dori's story hints at, and the ending I am
in some sense still awaiting, is an articulation of the magnitude of

having and then losing a life that is based on belonging to something larger than oneself. If this is an experience that is barely known and thus even less mourned than most in our North American society, what does its absence mean? As someone who grew up with such a collective life and identity but must mourn and abandon it because it has become corrupted, untenable, sacrificial, does one have a different experience from those whose redemptive fantasies never achieved social realization, for whom such ideals are always already lost? The gap left by such a loss strikes me at times as something unbearable, more so because it is a loss simply unknown and unintelligible to our individualist society.

Given that difference, we must also ask how intelligible Dori's experience would be to an analyst who grew up with nothing more collectively shared than a baseball team. We could circle back and imagine how Glenys might have experienced Li-an's aspirations differently in terms of collective versus individual. What if she could have more fully identified with the passion that lies in a fantasy of healing not merely the parents, but the collective, the society? I ask this not because I am seeking a pedestrian solution to the problem of analyst and patient working from different cultural standpoints but rather because I am interested in what is intelligible to us, available given the limits of our experiences of the social. How can what is not immediately intelligible to us become so? To see one's life as "a manifestation of a complex collective fantasy" is one kind of experience; to see one's life as a manifestation of some individual set of social and personal intersections is quite different. For one thing, the former constellation might mean that individuals are far more quickly recognizable to each other, accessible to identification, than in other instances. To manifest a fantasy that is readily intelligible as collective, one that is meant to embody socially mediated sacrifice and redemption on behalf of a greater whole seems to me different, though not entirely so, than to embody a set of passions, intentions, hopes, and dreams such as motherhood that are culturally shared but individually realized on behalf of just one or two beings. Isn't it interesting that Eyal recognizes his shared reality with Dori immediately, whereas Maura must work through a plethora of differences to come to her obvious commonality with Melissa?

In general, it might be important to recognize the difference between, on one hand, an interpellation involving racism, homophobia, normative heterosexuality, or perfect motherhood and, on the other, a set of ideas that position you as a hero, a founder of utopia, a defender of your community. The burden of sacrifice involved in being someone meant to save your people—one I can recognize having been raised to serve the people of the oppressed classes—is one side of such a shared narrative.* The other side, however, is the greater assurance of collective belonging and having an impact. My thoughts in reading Eyal's paper after the others was to wonder what kind of difference there is between mourning one's own inability to fulfill a ideal one has embraced as curative but discovered to be impossible and mourning a "god that failed," a system that reveals itself to demand sacrifices while betraying the ones who sacrifice for it.

Colliding or Colluding in the Shadow of Oppression

The thread of mourning I have followed from chapter to chapter becomes more entangled in the complexity of Orna Guralnik's vignette. As she writes about the effects of colonialism and racism, she unpacks the loss of intelligibility to oneself that occurs when the picture of oneself as other has been swallowed and incorporated, as when her patient has received an indigestible dose of hatred that becomes self-hate. Thus, there emerges what Layton (2006b) has described as an impoverishment of the mind caused by de-linking individuals from their socio-political contexts. This de-linking activates dissociative dynamics (Guralnik, 2007); it denies linguistic signification to ordinary experiences that might rattle the social order. Instead, melancholically foreclosed into the world of the abject, individuals lose their ability to feel fully present and personified. In the process of immigration and becoming a Black among Whites, one kind of intelligibility is lost, which necessarily engenders melancholy. And how can this melancholy be dealt with in psychoanalysis when what

---

* This narrative is in turn part of a larger web of narratives: European Jewry divided itself between those who embraced religion, Zionism, and socialism in the late 19th century.

has been lost was both a real world, lost through emigration, and a status that is created by the othering action of a discourse that cannot be individually resisted?

Ede's efforts at collective resistance turn out to be self-defeating, and Orna's efforts to educate her about the laws of the society she resists only intensify her spiral into loss of agency and fantasies of restitution. Not only is Orna representing the "Whiteness" from which Ede is excluded, but in this Black and White constellation Ede loses access to a part of Orna she desperately needs but perhaps does not know or hope for: a framework for action, for justice, that involves a viable lawfulness rather than the restitution sought in a helpless victimhood that despairs of any law but that of power (expecting the world to set right its wrongs). Perhaps this reflects my own theoretical predilection, but I confess I was most gripped by the moment of manifestation at which Orna seeks to bring the issues of economics and power, law and lawfulness into the smaller arena of the therapeutic relation. The law was so differently perceived, interpreted, intelligible to each of them, so differently privileging, yet they are able to negotiate these different realities in the arena of the third.

The question of whether there was a law that could regulate Ede's and Orna's relationship is answered by Orna with the description of a negotiated deal that involves responsibility and agency on both sides, hence a nascent form of mutuality: We show up, you pay, I accept what you give. This is an attempt to restore lawfulness, responsibility, to set up a moral third that creates boundaries and structures that could only be further destabilized by righteous acts of transgression—the kind that in the past left Ede disregulated. If I understand this sequence correctly, there is a consensual reality that can be embraced: Ede needs to pay; Orna needs to clean up her billing.

Before asserting this third Orna, we should emphasize, first—and I would say necessarily, inevitably—falls into what she describes as a failure, a lapse into judgment, lack of ability to understand Ede's relation to the system. Fair to the core, Orna suggests the limits of both her and Ede's view of the law, the bind they are in reflecting a truth about the system: It is corrupt, but it also corrupts and contaminates many an effort at resistance, which seeks to undo it. This is the fundamental dilemma in helping anyone to step out of victimhood. I would hold that Orna's task is not uncommon to any therapy involving trauma: Maintaining that most tenuous balance between representing in the enactment both the perpetrator who can admit the crime and the one who witnesses the crime and its acknowledgment. Being both the representative of that white society that needs to know what it has done to the Other, and the one who can identify with the intense pain of that other is a specific, intense version of a larger dilemma.

The perversion of the third, in the sense of third as social order or law, poses a specific problem for the therapist beyond what may be (and I am not so sure of this in Orna's case) her acceptance of a privileged legal and color position. As I (Benjamin, 2006) have elaborated on other occasions, the analyst's awareness of her failures in recognizing the hurt and reinflicting of old wounds causes her to have to struggle with self-regulation, with shame and guilt. I would argue that Orna's dual role, like that of any psychoanalytic therapist who unavoidably reactivates a patient's traumas and wounds, is of being witness as well as representative of the perpetrator. Holding both positions, standing in that space between, is a crucial part of cleaving to the moral third. Yet to witness as White places a different stress, a different kind of identification as perpetrator, and thus an even greater challenge to the therapist's efforts at self-regulation.

Thus, this dyad has many specific challenges posed by interpellation that compel a kind of guilt and struggle for the therapist of a specific kind. In her witness function she must do what the bystander mothers and women in Ede's family could not, insist on some kind of law. But at the same time, she must not fail as the White world does to recognize the injuries it inflicts. We learn that there is another issue related to law and lawfulness, another structure to contend with, that Orna tries to hold in mind: patriarchy, the exploitation of women as a fact of Ede's society of origin and not only her adopted colonial or White society. Orna needs to be a double witness, and accordingly she allows Ede to direct her most vehement and fierce outburst to an ambiguous You, who have let "the men" rape and deny me, treated me as garbage, and prevented my mother from speaking out to protect me.

This leads me to wonder if, without a shared consciousness of colonialism and patriarchy, a discursive awareness shared despite their differences, Ede could articulate this double oppression and betrayal by her own people as well as Whites, one that she could formerly only dimly, dissociatively endure. Without a consciousness of patriarchy, a sense of law that goes against the grain of race and with the grain of gender, in other words without the consciousness regarding incest and exploitation that feminism has brought about, Orna and Ede might have lost all bearings—and would surely have lost a crucial ingredient of the moral third. Perhaps Orna might have drowned in her Whiteness and Ede's victimhood without having any compass but guilt to feel her way through the differences in their lives.

This last remark on feminism returns us, not exactly full circle perhaps, to the matter of what kind of experiences are shared, mutually intelligible, rooted in collective fantasy. Even with this disparate pair, Orna and Ede, the goal of mutual intelligibility must be striven for, if not attained, precisely with the help of recognizing discursive practices and our cooperative efforts to resignify them. It is this tension between what is intelligible, resignifying, and meaning-giving on one side and what is oppressive and normative on the other that we struggle to bear in mind with these amazing and complex depictions of therapeutic consciousness of the role of discourse in their own and their patients' lives.

PART II

INTERPELLATIONS

7

RAVEN

Travels in Reality

ORNA GURALNIK

EDITOR'S INTRODUCTION

These essays are remarkable for their capacity to meld the immediacy of clinical work with theoretical reflections on the context and constraints of that work. Here, in regard to self and body, identity and race, and the analyst–patient relationship, Guralnik demonstrates how clinical reflection weaves with a focus on interpellation. Using "a kind of psychoanalysis infused with *ideology critique*," she tracks how an adolescent's rituals of tattooing and scarification interpellate the analyst as Other, a discursive site Guralnik agrees to inhabit by "develop[ing] a less possessive curiosity," even while making critique of this enlistment central to the analysis of her countertransference and its value in her work.

Before depositing their troubled daughter in my care, Raven's parents sat me down for an interview. Worried and fearful, they doubted her capacity to finish high school. Her mom imagined her failing to thrive, maybe a junkie who would never be able to let go of the apron strings. Indeed, during our first few sessions, Raven was disengaged, absent, directionless. Her body hidden under giant shreds of clothing, she maintained little eye contact and often abandoned sentences mid-air. It was hard to tell what, if anything, really bothered her: her failing grades, her flunking druggy boyfriend, her cell phone disconnected for the fourth time? Still, Raven and I wove our relationship easily. She was a gentle, smart, lovable, and confused kid. Much of our alliance relied on two simple ingredients: my not being frightened by her and practical advice on how to deal with intrusive parents. Occasionally, Raven let me in on troubles like school work, her "bi-curious" relationships, or her deeply loving but painful relationship with her mom. But mostly, polite and resigned, she was comfortable in a space of inarticulation, a place she could be caught owning nothing.

While I was getting to know Raven, a parallel plot was being inscribed on her exquisite biracial skin. In contrast to her mild, non-committal stance toward the world, her body art became increasingly radical: tattoos, nose and tongue studs, belly and nipple rings all came and went. She was contemplating flesh-hooking. I was hoping that this progression somehow indicated a strengthened voice rather than a deteriorating mental state. Raven was part of a subculture of kids who engage in wild play with their reality and identity. In addition to mind-altering substances or mosh-pit crashing, body practices such as scarification and flesh-hook suspension kept challenging the sanctity of the Natural and Real. Against the backdrop of regulatory pressures to respect the "destiny" of the *given*, *natural* body, these kids kept reconstructing the self as an object of will and fantasy (In Orlan's words: "I fight against God and DNA"; Knafo, 2009). How do we psychoanalytically theorize the wish to negotiate with reality?

Historically, body modification human practices date 5,000 years back to flesh-hooking rituals in India. In African and indigenous Australian cultures, cutting, scarification, and body modification were considered the ultimate mark of civilization, where transcendence and a "state of grace" were to be reached and the unseen world accessed through the body (Ooi, 2004). The body is used to transcend the body. The pursuit of limit experiences, preserved to this date, continues to take on our relationship to the Real and as a practice is a commentary on the proper state of consciousness.

In psychiatric lingo, we typically categorize Derealization as a disorder, an involuntary and highly disruptive state. Similarly, we conceptualize acts of "self-mutilation" as reenactment of past trauma, or a maladaptive attempt to break through depersonalization to get back to feeling "Real" (Fowler, 1999; Guralnik and Simeon, 2001). Radical body art turns this formulation on its head, exposing how one's past, and the reassuring constraints of regulatory discourse, can threaten the authentic experience of reality and personhood. Elsewhere (Guralnik and Simeon, 2010), I questioned the prevailing assumption that dissociation signifies a damaged self. For some, Normative Reality is far from being reassuring but is rather the source of psychic numbness and agitation. Body modification is all about the active pursuit of limit states, chasing the dragon of exit and rebirth, leaving us with the question: What is authentic experience?

In Raven's circles, scarification or flesh suspension were rituals kids took seriously as a hard-earned method to reach states of grace. About having been flesh-hooked above an audience of 10 peers, one of her friends said, according to Raven, "I can't tell you what happened while I was up there.... I ... remember, but ... can't explain. I had the most intense, incredible few minutes of my life.... Turning ... to see each arm stretched towards the horizons, I gathered my thoughts, and for the first time in over a year, I felt complete. Content with life, with myself, and with the world I now looked at from a completely different perspective."

Why did Raven have so little use for talking about stuff? She was raised by decent, devoted working-class parents. Her African American mom held a government job for decades, and her Ashkenazi Jew dad was slowly completing his college degree. Raven described them as deeply and anxiously committed to her brother and her yet oddly unable to address them. Her mom's speech was constricted and melancholic, the speech of a person trying to shield her family from history and pain. Her dad, fully compliant with mom's system, rarely offered any thirdness of narrative (Kristeva, 1998). Indeed, the stories of Raven's parents' unlikely meeting, their class, race, and religious differences, and their Romeo–Juliet breaks with their families were never narrated. Instead, they became hollowed by the lack of history and context and inaccessible to their children as full beings. Raven was left needing to find another venue to explore all this excess passed down to her. Her urges to mark her skin were often triggered when she was called to make verbal statements that categorized her: about her sexual orientation (You're dating a girl? Are you gay?), define her racial identity (does she sign up for a birth-right trip to Israel?), make educational choices that might position her in relation to her parents' socioeconomic class of origin (take financial aid to sponsor graduate school?). Language did not map well onto her experience. Instead, in response to such interpellative calls, she would slither back into derealization while continuing a liminal study of self—on her skin.

Raven was literally carving a space in which, as Strenger (2004) puts it, she could rewrite a narrative of self. Generation Y-ers, in Strenger's view, are preoccupied with renegotiating authorship over their life narrative. They abide by Friedrich Nietzsche's imperative to create the self, rather than just, as in the dominant ethos of our time, find it. No more of that *true self* hidden under imposed layers, but *true freedom* by shaping the materials of self into an aesthetically compelling creation. Michel Foucault (2005) viewed liminal experience as functioning to wrench the subject from itself: a project of desubjectivation and destruction.

***

A couple of years into our work, Raven moved into her college dorm while her brother, having joined the army, was sent to Iraq. Although highly liberal in their political affiliations, her parents were mainly relieved that their son was finally in a structured environment. Complying with family regulations, no one referred to any anxiety about his being in a chronic state of danger. Around then, Raven showed up with studs threaded through both forearms. The link was to be established only much later. She was proud and happy to have taken these on and then was crushed into helplessness by her mother's disgust. In contrast, I became the grown-up respecting her. I asked about the pain involved but was also genuinely moved by how beautiful and interesting the studs were. I was relieved to somehow manage to maintain my curiosity and not become alarmed. Two weeks later Raven was hospitalized with a severe infection of both arms.

How does one hold both worry for the integrity of a dear person's body and respect for her project of transcending that very same body? Body modification, from radical art to sex reassignment, never leaves the witness neutral. The witness is called to interpellate the act by taking a stand on health, social order, reality, and "true nature." Whose discourse was I to represent? Wasn't I to "understand"—systematize, categorize, perhaps pathologize, and target for "intervention"? In an attempt to remain open to new possibilities, I tried to develop a less possessive curiosity—not rush to categorize but give Raven a chance to imprint my mind-skin with what she was after. I knew the *show-ings* of the prized lacerations, bruises, holes, foreign metal objects, or glow-in-the-dark brandings had ceremonial qualities. What could be more Real than her oozing flesh? Yet what could be more of a spectacle, calling for interpretation? I mined my countertransference for clues: abjection, fascination, horror, and concern for Raven's well-being shared mental space with my admiration of her courage, pain tolerance, and pushing of the envelope.

I took inspiration from radical body artists, who voluntarily put their bodies through pain and self-mutilation and demand their audi-ence to tolerate these performances and grow with them. Marina Abramovic, Chris Burden, Bob Flanagan, and Orlan use their bodies as installation–performance pieces to make us contend with what we wish not to bear. Consider Stelarc, who *sewed shut his lips* and eye-lids and inserted cameras in his internal organs. In his body of work, Regular speech is Regulatory speech. He shuts up one register and turns to another to express the passion for the Real that is intensifying with the virtualization of our daily life. If we follow Stelarc, suspend our habitual ways of perceiving reality, what might we discover? Can we truly relinquish normativity?

And what about the frightening fact that letting go of normativity instantly exposes us to the distant thunder of *lawlessness*? As witnesses to body modification, we are thrown into a moral scene (Freund-Chertok, 2010). By joining the patient's or artist's act of freedom, we become passive participants in a horrific moment. What about the fact that Raven had to be hospitalized for weeks for a dangerous blood infection? The situation is paradoxical and "unresolvable." Any such identity collapses into meaninglessness without this dialectic. No tat-too or nipple ring will maintain its meaning outside the context of regulatory power, with which they are in dialogue. It is where inter-pellation and resistance spark, and this spark is the key, the portal to an alternate universe.

Analyzing the pressures of discourse around gender, race, class, and how these played out in Raven's parents' particular history took center stage in our work. Indeed, a kind of psychoanalysis infused with *ideology critique* was what most helped her mature and become more discerning in her relationships, a stronger and more self-directed student, and an avid world traveler. By the end of our third year, our work deepened significantly and brought about a few transformational episodes. After a year of service in Iraq, her brother returned to New York. Through Raven's reports, it was clear that he was severely traumatized. Of course, family-style, nothing was said. Raven was worried.

Orna: Does anyone ever ask him what he has been through?
Raven: No!
O: Why not?
R: He'd tell us if he needed to …
O: Do you ever ask him if he wants to talk about it?
R: No. I don't think I should! He'll talk when he is ready.
O: What if he understands this as his family not being ready to bear what he has to say?

   [Silence]

R: My mom thinks the most important thing is that we all stick together?
O: Who?
R: The three of us.

Soon Raven's brother stopped talking. For months he would only text. He was packing his stuff into boxes and had removed all of his pictures from the walls. He was leaving this world, and there was a big silence in that house. Thinking of her veteran brother's isolation was very difficult for me to bear. I was sad and outraged to realize Raven was reproducing the same family constraints on speech she herself was so affected by. When it comes to the State, we are all handcuffed. Pissed off with my attitude, Raven punished me with a 2-week hiatus and came back still furious. She was irate about my outright questioning of her family's sacred ideology of silence. We worked hard to break out of this enactment and find a place of mutual understanding that was ultimately transformative for both of us. This impasse illuminated how each of us was bound within the horizon of our sociopolitical context (Cushman, 1995). What can be spoken about, together, is not only decided by a particular dyad (parent–child or analyst–patient).

In this case, the destruction of an American soldier's life, and the life of his family, was not speakable here in the United States in 2007. Even deeper was how race and class interacted with the losses of war. I had to grapple with my naïve idealism and reckon with the protective/defensive powers of discourse. Raven's parents did not have the liberty of processing the disjuncture between the State's requirements for good citizenship and their dear son's trauma. Silence protected them all. Young Raven could not be the one to metabolize the burden of the profound rupture among her brother's individual experience, their parents, and the country that sent him to Iraq.

Radical body art occurs outside of language; the skin is injured when language falls apart. During this process Raven came with a new body mark that I immediately asked to see; this required her to peel off her trousers to reveal a giant oozing scar of a tree carved on her upper thigh and hip.

O: Ugh! That looks amazing!
R: Yeah, it was not as painful as it looks.
O: How did it feel?
R: You go into this trance. All I could do was focus on this tree and what it meant to me.
O: I can't help but feel bad for your skin. It is beautiful, but I wish you didn't hurt yourself.

[Raven stares at me—is it a medical gaze she will find? I am quiet.]

O: OK, but what does the tree mean to you?

I do not want to abandon Raven to her implicit search for meaning; I want to join her there with no judgment. The pairing of my insistence on making room for her brother's trauma and her narrative triggered a change.

R: It is naturally proud, and tall and big and wild and powerfully grounded to mother Earth. I believe in its life force.

Her eyes shone. I think of the dogged wars people incite and of the life-sustaining power of trees. Was Raven's brother the hoped-for root in the ground? Could his sacrifice be necessary to erase the shadows of past traumas of persecution and slavery?

I will conclude with Raven's dream, reported soon after the very last scarification or tattoo she ever did. She never connected the two, and neither did I. Upon leaving, already standing up and fidgeting with her big buckle, Raven turned to me: "I forgot to tell you. I dreamt about my brother. His face was full of shrapnel. Something horrible was happening to him. I came close to him and started hugging him; the shrapnel started coming out of his face. We kept getting closer; I couldn't hug him close enough. And it kept coming out, and I kept hugging him."

8

DARREN WITH DOMINIC

From the Social to the Psychic

STEPHEN HARTMAN

EDITOR'S INTRODUCTION

Hartman, a postmodern critic of gendered and sexed dichotomies, writes in a discourse that accepts gender as at once critique, social force, and personally meaningful entity. Negotiating this set of paradoxes or contradictions, he finds the conventional construal of gender to have great therapeutic power in his ongoing work with Darren: Just because gender is constructed doesn't mean it's not real. Equally wisely, he distinguishes two approaches to the problem of the psychic and the social. The first and more familiar strategy entails describing how the surrounding culture influences the person. In the second, "recursive" approach, "the psychic and the social are each wrapped in the momentum of the other." In Darren's case, Hartman's analysis of the social discourse of masculinity helps trace his patient's psychological use of social vectors, in the course of which restrictive essentialism slips into liberatory momentum.

Enactments between analyst and patient are sometimes illuminated by a jolt of political awareness. When the unconscious becomes conscious in these moments, we see just how saturated the mind is with social and cultural values, just how dissociated the link between the psychic and the social can be (Layton, 2006b), and just how important it is that that link be reestablished.

Once Darren and I began to map political zones in the erotic transference (see Chapter 2), it became easier to loop back to Darren's "psychodynamics." After we began to link questions of erotic possibility

75

with political intelligibility, matters of gender came into view, and we turned afresh to Darren's internal experience of gender. We noticed how Darren's experience of dependence registered split-off anxieties about gender roles that were harbored in his parents' unconscious. I return to my work with Darren here to show how the psychic and the social reveal one another in a recursive relation, each continuously mirroring and transforming the other. The upshot is that, in the early phase of treatment, political constraints on desire were revealed in the erotic transference. As our work progressed, we traced the arc of Darren's "object choice" moving past the politics of gay marriage to my role as Darren's mother.

So, fast-forward: Darren is in love. He and Dominic have moved in together. After years of being chronically and inexplicably single, Darren has a truly special love: a wonderful man who is an exciting lover and a devoted partner. Darren's apartment now furnished in fashionable mid-century modern (Darren's) and quirky Long Island Italianate (... um, er, *his*). Darren has become more or less relaxed about the pairing. He found a man who is not the authorized Chelsea version, a man who treasures tchotchkes that would have once made Darren shriek. Just home from a convention in Las Vegas, Dominic arrives with flowers wearing a tacky airport souvenir knit. Darren laughs. He feels loved—plus he gets to strip off that "lousy T-shirt." Dominic is no fool. If ever a big lug could win the nervous heart of a well-scrubbed hipster. The headboard is banging. Marriage is not far off. Darren and Dominic have a way of trading roles—gay-guy with guy-guy with girly-guy—that had long seemed as improbable to Darren as Dominic's San Gennaro medallion on his George Nelson nightstand.

The problem I turn to now is how to work with the social category, gender, in its "intrapsychic" mirror. One way, a more traditional way, is to elaborate a connection between elements of a person's psychic structure and points of cultural reference. One gathers how culture influences psychology (i.e., a needy man is at odds with our culture's esteem for male agency). Here, the interface of the psychic and the social describes ways that the internal experience of a person comes into conflict with the cultural surround. This view retains the notion that the psychic and the social are relatively autonomous parts of knowing. Rather, I am inclined to search for ways culture and psychology continually penetrate and reinvent one another. This approach sees the analysis of a person's psychic life unfolding within an analysis of social discourse and also traces the vector of social experience through the narration of a person's psychological life. Following the example of many feminist authors and theorists like Edgar Levenson (1983) and Muriel Dimen (2003, 2011), for whom clinical experience and clinical theory are recursive, here the psychic and the social are each wrapped in the momentum of the other: inside shaping outside shaping inside shaping outside. The only way one can know the psychic and the social is by continual reference by each to the other.

And, so, fast-forward. Darren's heart is broken—but not by love. A congenital heart disease that killed his mother has manifest. A surgery that was not available to her saved him. Without Dominic constantly at his bedside, he tells me, he is not sure he would have survived.

It is not so simple to have the man of your bed become the caretaker at bedside. Surrogate wife was Darren's role during his mother's decline while she expressed ever more contempt for feminized need and feminine care. The lonely mother spent her final years determined to cultivate an aura of independence. She became increasingly androgynous as her illness drained her of dignity as her husband cowered in an increasingly feminized retreat. Angry Darren commanded his father to "stop being a pussy." The father's salvo: "Was that a punch or a slap?" Masculinity and femininity were taking a beating. Celibate by mother's bedside, Darren was more Xeno the Stoic than Oedipus. In an unspoken contract with her not-yet-out gay son, Mother showed no signs of pain and he none of homosexuality. Weakness was not in order. She felt castrated and became castrating. He felt panic. The best he could do was emulate her misogyny and disavow his need for her to mother. Sexual excitement was banished. Father, unable to cope, hides in his office. Ailing mother appears self-sufficient and proud. Son, captain of the wrestling team, flaunts ripped biceps nervous that his love muscle will tweak in his singlet. Father lords over Darren's imagination as Bruce Webber at an Abercrombie and Fitch photo shoot: fashioning masculinity with a keen eye to its feminine sculpting. After Mother died, Darren came out. But he could never find a respectable lover whose masculinity wasn't always at risk. Darren and I play married and wannabe until the container of gay normality cracks.

Darren arrives to the session in a state of panic. It is reasonable that he would feel anxious after surgery his doctor tells him, and he could relax. But he can't. He can't stop feeling like a pussy himself. "I have always taken solace in my body," he tells me. "I was a wrestler with washboard abs. I want to be running on the beach in Provincetown flaunting my strength. But do you see this paunch!" he laughs. "What am I to do!" I'm glad that he is laughing, and I ask about Dominic. "Ah …," he sours. "I loved having him take care of me. But something about it made me uncomfortable. I just about lost it when he wanted to have sex in the hospital. Are you kidding me?" Darren says to me as if making it clear to Dominic that your analyst can't be your lover. "Why not?" I ask, aware that he is restraining me as well. Darren thought it too feminine to be attended to and, also, seduced. "Huh?"—me, and then we both laugh.

We recall that Darren's mother had utter disdain for need; care is most safe when androgynous. Darren has been in analysis long enough to postulate that he was identified with the sick mother's rejection of the depressed father's sexual ambiguity. Father couldn't reassure her in a way that would establish masculine order. Darren's withdrawal to the sickly position met Dominic's assertive mix of care and desire with confusion and shame. Darren's ambivalence at Mother's bedside, his need for Father's strength and rage at mother's strictures against weakness have led him to accept neither mothering nor fathering easily. Masculinity and femininity seem both out of reach. Homosexuality seems too often the flimsy version of each— "Just look around." Darren tries to get me to join him in a moment of gay bashing as if that would settle his nerves. I raise an eyebrow with a calculated mixture of curiosity and camp and, then, switch tactics. "Dominic doesn't seem to give a fuck about weakness," I suggest. "He's immune to it somehow, isn't he?" "Yes, he is blessed!" says Darren, smiling now calmly.

I fall in love with Dominic more every day. I don't know how he managed to elude the dramas of passing, which plague so many of us, but he manages to transcend fixed gender categories with remarkable ease. Is it because he grew up in a traditional environment that knew no Oscar Wildes and valued family full-stop? Or is it that he isn't gender troubled in quite the same way? I picture him at Darren's bedside in the recovery room unworried that the moment will soon arrive when the law requires he, the illegal wife-man, must surrender the position at bedside to Darren's brother, the authorized man-man, who arrives to speak on Darren's behalf. Dominic is just as aloof to the interpellations of the scene—fag at unconscious lover's bedside— as to the introjects that Darren, deeply unconscious, must surely be entertaining in his deep slumber: son with mother in the place of father now as a desiring subject. In Dominic's care, I observe, Darren is brought more fully into being. Dominic may not be a gender theorist, and he is surely an old-fashioned kind of guy, but, for Darren, he is a potent warrior for a transgendered normativity.

My role in the transference is shifting. I am still sometimes a married doctor modeling acceptability and still sometimes a model lover. I am often called upon to scowl at anything that reeks of gender variance. More often, I feel like the m-t-f trans hero played eponymously by Candace Kane on the primetime show *Dirty Sexy Money*. She relishes kissing Billy Baldwin in the back seat of his limo. Caught in the act, he confronts his father, Donald Sutherland: "*She* is more of a man than you'll ever be." As caretaker, worthy lover, and desiring subject myself, I take on masculine and feminine roles that recursively allow Darren to break apart the fixity of gender categories that had alienated his parents from each other's affection.

Soon I will have to give up Darren so that he can be with "an appropriate object." Whoever might imagine that postmodern psychoanalysts don't worry about resolving Oedipal dynamics misses the point. We do—but in a perpetual meeting of the psychic with the social and the social with the psychic.

9
GLENYS
White or Not

GLENYS LOBBAN

EDITOR'S INTRODUCTION

Lobban's account of discovering her racial heritage, whose clinical reverberations will become apparent in Part III, shows forcefully how a "cultural category ... impacts subjectivity." Here we see how mind needs society, taking it in as, in this instance, it also takes it on. As Lobban processes multiple new, and injurious, interpellations that come her way, she reflects on her own participation with them. Discovering the plethora of discursively constituted racial stereotypes she did not know she carried, she fights fire with fire. Using Butlerian theories of social discourse, she elects to own the essentialist caricatures abjecting her and thereby reempowers herself.

The construction of personal identity is "a complex, continuing affair in which we are inscribed by culture in a myriad of contradictory ways" (Rivera, 1989, p. 28). These cultural inscriptions are powerful and difficult to shift, but they are not indelible. Psychoanalysis can provide a context for their interrogation and facilitate what Butler (1997) terms "resignification." In this chapter I will dissect a specific example of cultural inscription: the development of racialized subjectivity.

The scene: Sunday lunch in sunny, post-Apartheid, Cape Town, South Africa, in the year 2004. A barbeque, what South Africans call a *braai*, is in progress in a garden rich with vivid tropical flowers, the distant roar of the Atlantic Ocean in the background. Present are the members of a "White" South African family: two siblings, Margaret and Bill, both in their 80s, Bill's wife, many children and grandchildren. It is a family reunion. Nobody mentions the backdrop: Margaret has metastasized breast cancer and is beginning to ail. The desultory conversation turns to their British ancestors who were lured out to Africa by gold's siren song.

Suddenly, Margaret sits up ramrod straight. "We always talk about the English relatives, the paternal ancestors. It is time we paid attention to my mother's side of the family. She was extraordinary after all. It is pretty unusual to have a mother who is a medium and gifted with second sight. I've decided that today is the time to admit the truth about our mother's family." (Her brother, Bill, shifts uncomfortably in his garden chair, almost demurs.) "This is about Adinah, my mother's mother, who died before I was born. Well, the truth is that she, Adinah, my maternal grandmother, was 'Colored'."

Conversation skids to a halt. Later, there is a barrage of questions from some of the family members. Margaret explains that she figured out from hints her mother dropped that Adinah was Colored. She never told anyone the secret during the Apartheid years because it wasn't safe. If the authorities had discovered that Margaret and Bill were one-quarter Colored, they would have forced them to move out of their White neighborhood and sent them to a Colored school and their parents could not have remained married.

As the sun is setting and the shadows in the garden lengthen, Margaret produces two faded sepia photographs of Adinah taken in the 1890s. In one, Adinah is a passenger in a wagon drawn by four oxen en route from Cape Town to the goldfields. The other is a traditional family portrait, taken in Johannesburg, of Adinah, her husband and children. Family members pour over the photos. "What do you think? Could this story of Margaret's be true?" "Maybe she's getting senile." "Bill doesn't seem to believe it." "I think Adinah looks Colored in the photo." "How can you tell skin color when the photo is brown and white?" "Well, look at her hair in the photo, even pulled back in a bun you can see that it is extremely curly." "Wow, I think it would be cool to be part 'Black'."

There is some debate about how to define Colored. The youngest grandchild has been educated in post-Apartheid South Africa. She tells them that the Coloreds are descended from the mix of different slaves from India, West Africa, and East Africa, who were brought to the Cape by the Dutch East India Company in the 1700s. These slaves partnered up with each other, White settlers and Black South Africans, making the Coloreds a truly multicultural group. "I learned all this when my class visited the Slave Lodge Museum where the slaves lived," she says. "It made me so sad. Slavery was South Africa's secret that we never acknowledged during Apartheid."

The tone of the gathering shifts; discomfort and uneasiness are in the air. Rapid goodbyes are said. "Well," says Margaret, "I had a great time. I feel so much lighter, relieved of my burden." Following the *braai* Bill dismisses his sister's news, explaining: "That's just Margaret, always trying to find a way to be center stage."

Margaret's condition worsened rapidly, and she died 2 years later.

I am Margaret's daughter. I was present at the party when she revealed our family's secret. Initially, I was thrilled to hear that I had a Colored great-grandmother. I fought against Apartheid in South Africa in my youth, and later I left South Africa to escape my automatic White privilege. Now I could feel truly part of the New Rainbow Nation of South Africa, more of an "us" than a "them." Some of my White South African friends were envious; they joked that I was lucky I could unload my White South African guilt.

A year after my mother died, I decided to have my mitochondrial DNA tested in South Africa. It turned out that my mother's story was true. The lab director who informed me about my results explained that my DNA showed that I am not White—I am "Eurasian," a mix of European and Asian. The most likely explanation for my DNA is that I am a descendent of a slave, a woman who was brought to Cape Town from South East Asia sometime in the 1700s. My closest current genetic matches are individuals in India, Sri Lanka, and the Maldives. They expect to find other South African matches for me when the database grows larger.

So, at age 57, I discovered that I am not all White after all. I am one-eighth Colored. When I was hailed as Eurasian by the lab director, this triggered a complex set of affective reactions for me. Their intensity surprised me, especially given that this discovery had no material impact on my life. I continue to be seen as all White by everyone I meet, and I continue to enjoy the privilege and power of "Whiteness." My feelings were very intense, yet they were almost entirely internal, as my change of status did not seem to register with anyone else. My subjectivity and discourse were entangled in a strange internal contretemps. I decided to try to render my affects in words because they are a concrete example of how the cultural category of race impacts subjectivity.

The first thing that I noticed after I got the results of my DNA test was that I lost my subjective experience of Whiteness. I found out that I was not all White, but I felt that I was not White at all. Joni Mitchell's words kept going through my head: "Don't it always seem to go that you don't know what you've got till it's gone?" Apparently I absorbed the "one-drop rule" (Broyard, 2007, p. 66) that operated in Apartheid South Africa (and the American South), which stated that one drop of "non-White" blood defines a person as "not White."

In Apartheid South Africa, Whiteness was the gold standard. Whiteness, like the power and privilege accompanying it, was reserved by law for those who were all White. South Africans were divided into different categories based on skin hue. Race was the currency that bought privilege and power; it even trumped class. People who were classified as Black formed 80% of the population and were at the bottom of the hierarchy, followed by the Coloreds who were 9% of the population. Whites were at the apex of power and controlled the political and cultural apparatus, though they were only one-tenth of the populace. Negative stereotypes about Whiteness and those who were not White were part of the dominant discourse that shaped me (on the psychic dimensions of Whiteness, see Altman, 2000, 2004, 2006; Harris, 2007a, 2007b; Layton, 2006a; Straker, 2004, 2006, 2007; Suchet, 2004, 2007).

Shortly after I heard my DNA results I registered a huge dip in my self-esteem. I began to feel depleted and depressed. Eventually I realized what had caused these feelings. I was interpellated by the lab director (Dimen, this volume). The director at the DNA lab hailed me as Eurasian, as not White, and I began viewing myself through that lens. I noticed that when negative events occurred, such as the unreasonable bank teller yelling at me, I'd think to myself, "He's doing that because he can see that you aren't really White." I no longer experienced myself as cushioned by my Whiteness with the self-esteem, confidence, and entitlement that go along with that. Instead, my positive self-esteem was leached out; I felt like an outsider, unimportant, and unentitled.

I discovered that I possessed a wide array of racist stereotypes. These popped up as soon as I was hailed Eurasian, and, once interpellated by my DNA test, I began applying them to myself. It was interesting how these stereotypes and my gender intersected. I experienced myself via my set of images pertaining to powerless "Indian" or Colored South African slave women, and that further eroded my self-esteem. Six months after my DNA test, I visited the Slave Lodge Museum in Cape Town. I was tremendously upset by the stories about how the female slaves (my ancestors) were physically and sexually abused and powerless to resist. This information added to my ammunition against myself. I began to feel older, less attractive, careworn, invisible, powerless, a downtrodden beast of burden who was good only for cooking and serving men. I was shocked by the depth of my feelings and how futile it was to try to apply reason to them.

I dreamed that I found my dog from childhood, a white Maltese terrier, lying injured on the lawn, in pieces like Humpty Dumpty. I was trying to put her back together. Following this dream, I put on my analyst hat and diagnosed myself. I concluded that I was having my own version of the "racial melancholia" that Eng and Han (2000) describe. I was experiencing myself as "mixed," "not White," "part South Asian," and it was painful to have lost my familiar White self and the ideal of Whiteness.

Fortunately, even as my White self was experiencing all this *Sturm und Drang*, my mother self, my analyst self, and random other selves soldiered on, albeit with the self-esteem gauge teetering on empty. Thank God for multiplicity (see Bromberg, 1998).

Once I had diagnosed my racialized subjectivity, I enlisted my analyst self to ponder what "resignification" (Butler, 1997) would look like for me. How could I interrogate and rework the label Eurasian so that it would no longer make me feel inferior? How to redefine "not White" and paint my own multiple, exotic definitions of "mixed"/"multi"/"rainbow"? A story in the *New York Times* that summed up the paradoxical essence of resignification provided me some creative encouragement at that moment. During the 2008 Democratic presidential primary, then-Senator Barack Obama was asked by a journalist how he felt about the fact that a historian had found evidence that he and Dick Cheney, the Republican vice president, were distant cousins. Obama replied that perhaps every family has to have its one "black sheep." In his humorous reply, Obama resignified the term "black sheep," and turned it on its head when he used it ironically to describe Mr. Cheney.

I started down my road to resignification when I decided to write this chapter. Today my lexicon has expanded: When I think of myself as Eurasian, positive traits like beauty, fortitude, strength, resilience, and intelligence come to my mind. Initially I was a reluctant traveler, but now I am very excited about the rest of my journey.

10

DAVID AND JONATHAN

The Hostility of Discourse

EYAL ROZMARIN

EDITOR'S INTRODUCTION

In Rozmarin's view, words are the property of history and culture, not the individual. He furthers his work on the individual and the collective by showing how the analyst, attempting to create meaning, inevitably stumbles into "meaning-making practices" that are antagonistic to patient or analyst or treatment. Writing of two patients' marriages, one gay and one straight, his thinking with them about these events reveals that one patient's imprisoning interpellation may be another's empowerment. With these cases, he illustrates the process by which the therapist invites patients to join in collective thought and, whatever the patient chooses to do, thereby to create a third position—of thought, shared process, history—in which meaning is made and examined.

Two of my patients got married this year. One of them married a man; the other married a woman. Since both of these patients are men, there were some obvious differences between the two weddings. David married his girlfriend, Shira, in a religious ceremony, followed by a big celebration hosted by proud parents. Jonathan married his boyfriend, Ronen, in a Canadian city hall. At the party a few weeks later there were many friends and family on Jonathan's side, but his new husband's family was absent. But it is not the marriages themselves that I'd like to discuss; it is rather the way they were conceived, or more accurately, what happened between proposal and acceptance. Needless to say, both men brought their stories to therapy, calling on me to take a position.

In retrospect, I can say that I found myself in an uncharted territory: an intersection, of sorts, between the wish for collaborative thought—or in other words, thirdness—and resistance to such collaboration. I mean these terms in a straightforward sense—thirdness, as for example in Jessica Benjamin's work (2006), resistance as in traditional psychoanalysis. But I also mean them conversely: the unconscious meaning of thirdness as a dyadic instance of collective thought and, as such, an agent of general social discourse versus what is sometimes a necessary resistance to the oppressive effects of such discourse. What I'd like to propose, with this dual meaning in mind, is that there is no such thing as a neutral conversation. Even as we attempt to create a position from which to contemplate subjective experience without preconceived notions, we find that there is no such position. We cannot but employ words and meaning-making devices that carry with them, in or outside consciousness, specific and sometimes hostile histories and ideologies. What do we do when thinking together feels and really is dangerous?

Jonathan is a 30-year-old Israeli who lives in New York. He met his future husband on a visit to Israel. Having just come out of a string of disappointing affairs, he was not looking for a relationship. But when he met Ronen, it was special. Within a few months Ronen came to live with him. Not long after, Jonathan came into my office and said, "We are going to get married!" It turned out that on a mundane weekend evening, Ronen asked, "Do you think we should get married?" "Of course," Jonathan replied, and took out his Blackberry. By the time he and I met the next evening, they had already set a date and figured out the entire procedure. I felt happy for him and was quick to say so. But at the same time it all seemed to me too rushed, too matter-of-fact, and I found myself uneasy and worried. I had no doubt that the relationship was good for him. Yet I could not see why there was such a rush to make it formal, except to counteract deep anxieties left in him by parents whose love was never certain. We should discuss this, I thought, explore the anxieties that had to be so fiercely overridden by action—action, moreover, that felt more like a plan for war than a pleasurable stage in a romantic union. Toward the end of the session I decided to speak: "It's a bit fast, don't you think?" I said. Jonathan replied, "No, I don't think so. We love each other; what is there to wait for?" The plan proceeded. But if he did not wish to question his marriage, Jonathan very much wanted to share it. And share it we did, all the way to the party in Tel Aviv, to which I was invited and happily attended.

David, my other patient, has just turned 35. He has also been unhappy in love, alone, or ambivalent about the women he had been dating. But when he met Shira the affair quickly became serious. A few months in, while on a romantic getaway, Shira brought up the topic of marriage. She did it very much like Ronen did; she asked David if he thought that they should, at some point, get married. But David's response was different: He froze and for a long moment could not say a word or feel anything. When he finally came back, all he felt was intense anger and a deep sense of betrayal. "What do you think happened to you?" I asked, confused by what seemed like a paradox. "We had such a beautiful love," he said, "a love that is only ours. And now she wants to bring all of society between us!" This, made sense. "You're right," I said. "Marriage really is the moment where love becomes the affair of society." "Yes," David replied, "we need to talk about it."

David and Shira got into an earnest dialogue about the meaning of marriage. During that time he tried to understand himself, to understand her, and to make sense of their sudden conflict. He loved Shira and respected her wishes, but what she saw as promising he saw as dangerous. *He* needed to trust that their relationship could withstand what seemed to him an invitation to overbearing intrusion. He gained this trust when Shira told him—and it was out of love, not out of exasperation—that if he needed *not* to marry to feel safe she would not dream of insisting.

Two very different spaces between proposal and acceptance, and likewise, two different spaces opening up, or not, in therapy. For Jonathan, question and answer grip each other like two sailors on a small boat on the high seas, facing a storm they could only survive together. And in such emergency, resistance to anything but me immediately joining—as if saying: You're either with us or against us, and if you're with us, jump on board without questions. For David the question itself summons the prospect of a dreadful storm, which is sure to come if he agrees to get married. What *he* asks of his future spouse, and of me, is to assure him that the storm could be weathered. But for him to feel so, neither she nor I can jump on board too quickly. We must each first deliberate and then take the right side in a battle where the individual and society are antagonistic. As if *he* is saying: If you're with us without questioning, you must be against us! Why this radical difference?

There are differences between these two men that usually come under the term *psychological*. These are, of course, relevant. But my purpose here is to reflect on another register in which all of this happened and continues to happen. It is the register in which Jonathan, a gay man, was determined to marry another gay man and, in that gesture, took a precarious position vis-à-vis the complex social discourse through which love relations are made intelligible and legitimate—a register in which David, a straight man, hesitated to marry a woman in fear of being crushed under the weight of tradition inherent, for him, in that gesture. It is the register, in other words, in which the meaning of subjective life clearly appears, in direct relation, to social possibilities and restrictions. In this register, what Jonathan aspired for David feared; what propelled Jonathan from the outside as an alluring frontier, threatened David from the inside like the gravitation of an overdetermined center. Yet, for some reason, paradoxically again, in this register: David trusted our ability to think together, while Jonathan felt it could only work against him.

We have in psychoanalysis an almost absolute faith in thought; we believe that thinking is better than thoughtless action. Even as we, hopefully, abandon the premise that what the analyst thinks is true and what the patient refuses to think is a sign of pathology, we still believe—in contemporary terms—that thirdness is better than enactment. But what these two stories perhaps demonstrate is that what appears to some of us as an ideal—the freedom of reflection from a third position can appear to others as a nightmare of hostility and antagonism. If David had trust in our ability to think together, Jonathan had about this prospect a profound sense of danger. Rightfully, since in many ways, the discourse we could have used does not allow his love a positive social meaning. If we were to seriously talk, we could not have ignored the many forms of shame and abjection evoked regarding homosexual love in history and contemporary politics. We could not have reflected about his motives except for within a framework that makes them questionable in principle. We *could have* talked about his wishes from a position of informed defiance, strive for resignification, as Judith Butler would have it (1997). But Jonathan did not wish to take a personal journey through queer and postmodern theory. He wanted to take a subjective stand that still does not have good and stable discursive coordinates. In this regard, thinking *would* have been an adversary. If he wanted to get there, resistance was necessary—he had to keep on rowing. David felt differently because, in his case, the two of us thinking together did not imply existential danger. It did not imply straying into discursive terrains that so thoroughly unsettle his subject position, or the possibility of his union. For him, thirdness held the promise of intelligibility and reason. He did not see collective thought as hostile to his project, even as he was paralyzed with dread of the collective pressure gathering around him.

Marriage is of course, as David knew, a glaring crossroad of subjective will and social power. But I believe the stories I have told you are dramatic instances of what happens in every therapeutic hour. The therapist invites the patient to join him in collective thought, to create a third position from which to address their singular and joint realities. In every given moment, the patient has the option of accepting or declining. But the third position has a collective unconscious. Words are heavy with history and culture. Thought itself is always, in a sense, an enactment of social and historical struggles. Every conversation has an unthought known, full of possibilities but also shame, anxiety, and violence.

This is why when the patient resists thinking; he might be fighting for a not yet possible to articulate yet meaningful survival. He may be asking for our help to stay afloat, when words and concepts feel as if they aim to drown him. The question for the therapist then becomes this: join the patient or abandon; when insisting on collective thought is a betrayal of the patient to antagonistic meaning-making practices, and accepting his resistance means joining in a shared position that is as important as it is unsafe to think about.

Or to put it differently: Sometimes, we can make a third of words; sometimes it requires going to the party.

11

AMY

The Intersection of Body and History

OLGA PUGACHEVSKY

EDITOR'S INTRODUCTION

When a clinician discovers she shares an experience with a patient, the discovery has a profound effect, whether she tells her patient or not. Pugachevsky's account of her journey with Amy registers the effect of social forces as they take place in both historical time and clinical time. In this instance, intergenerational transmission of trauma became key, but only after Pugachevsky understood that she, like her patient, was interpellated as the family's designated mourner. The analytic dyad, tossed about in the wake of the Holocaust, finishes its tragic voyage with an incomplete ending.

Knowing, not knowing, knowing for a fact, knowing as owning one's meaning, knowing in one's bones, collective knowing, the price of knowing and not knowing …

Amy, an attractive, 27-year-old, successful professional and a devoted girlfriend, wanted to fix one last thing she found to be not quite right in her well-ordered, crispy clean life—her inability to achieve an orgasm. She wanted to be done by the time of her usual summer vacation. So she went to her gynecologist first, then to a recommended sex therapist, and after that failed—to me. At our first meeting Amy explained concisely how she tried to find at least 15 minutes every day for what she called her "masturbation exercises," how it was so boring that she got into a habit of reading a book while doing it, and how, because her clitoris and labia began to hurt in about 12 minutes, she had to stop. My question—was she imagining anything sexual during

93

those 12 minutes?—got me an indignant glare and an angry statement that she had never had a "dirty" fantasy in her life.

You see, for Amy, her body was a property, sort of like a car, and
she wanted to learn what amounted to good parallel–parking skills.
Her soul had nothing to do with it. And that had to be challenged.
So I told my angry, not yet a patient (because I was not sure she was
coming back) that she should try to invent herself a sexual fantasy.
Amy asked if there was any other way.

To this I replied that I would need to know more before I could answer.
With surprise, Amy responded that she already told me everything.

"No," I said, "I mean about your history, your life in general, you
as a person."

"But what does it all have to do with my orgasm?" said she.

So Amy could tell me every detail about what used to be called one's
"private parts," but she wasn't ready to tell me where she was born.

Still she took out her pen and notebook and asked me for instructions on how to create a sexual fantasy. I gave her some.

Amy did come back. She came back because she was seriously
alarmed. "I tried, but my fantasy does not go beyond the PG rating
so to speak. I can imagine a dinner, a kiss, and then, right away, the
morning after. But my fantasy—it's all wrong," she said.

Thus, we started working in the good old way, by trying to articulate
Amy's lived world and her way of being in it as an embodied subject.

As Amy began to trust me more, the glossy initial picture of her
life—a neat house in the suburbs, two very loving parents, a mischie-
vous younger sister, two sets of also very loving grandparents somewhere in Florida, no problems at school, work, lots of friends, began
to acquire depth. Amy was a bit high-strung, a bit of a neat freak, a
bit of a health nut. Her mother seemed to be a very fragile vulnerable
creature, and Amy's job, as long as she remembered herself, was to
stand by her father and protect her mom from any worry or aggrava-
tion. It was also Amy's job to call all her grandparents every week.
And then there was her body to tend.

A description of the physical signs of sexual arousal, which I gave
to Amy one day, both appalled and unsettled her.

"It sounds like you are not quite comfortable with our corporeal
existence—all the mess of it," I said.

"Well," she said after a pause, "I don't think it's so much about the mess, though it's that too, but it's more like about people being so fragile, getting sick, and being in pain, and then, then, we all die."

After that session Amy had a nightmare.

"I am walking in a meadow covered with bright green grass. I am alone. Suddenly I see a deep pit full of mud right in front of me. There is a girl in the pit who can't get out. I pull her out, but it's not very easy because she is very heavy and slides back into the mud once or twice. Then I notice that I am all dirty too, and in the dream I am very upset. The girl looks like a grown-up, like somebody my age, but when I ask her, she says that she is 13."

"And what comes to mind when you think about the dream?" I asked.

"I don't know," she said. "It was really creepy. (pause) I know that I think of sickness and death more than other people. They just somehow don't think about it at all. I don't know how you can do it, with so many people dying every day. And you don't know when it can happen to you; it might be already happening to you. You might already have a tumor or something and not know about it."

I gently waited, and she continued.

"You know, my parents, they are also different. When I want to do something, like skiing or scuba diving, they don't say 'no,' but they send me these newspaper articles, statistics, you know, on how many divers, or skiers, die in accidents every year."

"And does it work?"

"Actually, yes, most of the time."

Amy laughed, an unhappy little laugh.

"It sounds very stupid, but you know, I still try not to have any arguments with my sister over the phone. And I do it with my parents and grandparents too."

"Sort of trying to keep your accounts in order just in case?"

"Sort of."

So Amy's world was one of unpredictable disaster always waiting around the corner, in which one's body signified no possibility of joy but only of pain, sickness, and death.

I don't have the space here to describe our explorations of the next few months. Suffice it to say that it felt like we investigated every angle, and still a dark shadow was holding both of us—and neither of us knew what it was.

So I went and presented the case in my then weekly supervision. "Is she Jewish?" he asked. Astonished, I said, "Yes." Then he said that one word—"Holocaust"—and my countertransference became clear as day.

Like Amy, I am the designated mourner in the third generation of the Holocaust survivors. But until my encounter with her, this role had always been just a fact. I had shunned the inherited task of creating a meaning out of the partial narrative, which was held both sacred and too horrendous to be told in full. Muted, it seeped into our everyday life through the cracks of language, preoccupations with pain and sickness, fears of loss, and the different ways every family member chose to defend themselves against those fears.

Actually these are all classical themes for the second generation of the Holocaust survivors (Adelman, 1995; Kestenberg, 1980; Wilson, 1985), but they are also relevant for those in the third generation who are stuck with the unprocessed trauma handed down to them. The collective history weighing upon both of us shadowed the very ways we structured our existence. In Amy's case, it literally seeped into her bones.

Now I was ready. I wasn't sure if Amy was. But she surprised me. She had been thinking about it too.

"OK, OK, all four of my grandparents are Holocaust survivors. And they always told me things. I had nightmares about camps and guards with dogs, and sometimes there were Jews there whom I couldn't save. My parents said that I just had a too vivid imagination; maybe I do. Never wanted to talk about what happened, just said that it was a long time ago and that I should not think about it so much. But you can't stop thinking about it. It's weird, you don't want to think about it, but you don't want it to be forgotten either. Like you want to remember. So when I was around 13 I actually videotaped all my grandparents telling their stories. Don't know why, but I thought it would make me feel better. Well, it did not, only made things worse."

Like the girl in her nightmare, Amy was 13 when she got all of the facts. But of course, she needed not a list of facts but a full meaningful narrative that she could make her own (Wilson, 1985)—a different kind of knowing. So we started on a new journey. I learned how

Amy's maternal grandmother managed to survive in Auschwitz and how her maternal grandfather happened to be in the backyard when Nazis came, heard his mother screaming, and managed to hide in a shed, and how during a mass execution her paternal grandfather jumped into the pit before he was shot, and escaped at night, and how her paternal grandmother survived just because she was a very pretty blond child and happened to play at the neighbors when Nazis came, so the same neighbors hid and later adopted her.

So we moved back and forth between past and present, telling, retelling, reliving, trying to create new meanings, new world. As in her dream, Amy was pulling herself out of the communal grave, sliding in the mire, falling down, getting up again. She was changing too, becoming less afraid, more curious, not holding her breath any more for the impending disaster.

It was about 10 months later that Amy burst into my office, with the words "OK, I did it!" which took me a moment to understand, since we hadn't talked about the big "O" in a while. It also took me a couple of minutes to realize that she was not happy but on the contrary very angry. With me!

"I am saying I am not doing it again, and nobody can make me. I don't know why people want it at all, to be so out of control. And you! Why didn't you tell me that it's really like the earth moves! Besides, even if I get used to it, I might get to like it so much that I will forget all my obligations and become a slut."

Amy left that day and never came back.

12

ANONYMOUS

Floaters

MAURA SHEEHY

EDITOR'S INTRODUCTION

The particularity of clinical work has wide-ranging relevance. Here Sheehy elaborates her understanding of maternal subjectivity by shifting from clinical detail to discursive understructure. Exploring the subject's dilemma—twinned reaching for and resistance to interpellation—she wonders whether the crisis of maternal subjectivity may be illuminated by Bhabha's concept of "hybridity." "Mothers need this term," she claims, judging from her own experience of the "Venn diagram of self-states" she has discovered with each child. Using "emergent maternal subjectivity," she articulates what is perhaps a general dilemma: "Becoming a mother happens simultaneously from without and within, like a hallucination. It is a part of the self that is more than a self-state. But what is it?"

Recently I had a call from a woman referred to me by a midwife I know. She said she was pregnant and having an eye problem: floaters, bits of protein floating around in her eye fluid that can be caused by pregnancy, are terribly annoying, and for which there is no treatment. "I've never been to a counselor before," she said over the phone, "but I tend to be an anxious person anyway, and this is making me really anxious. I thought I should talk to someone so I can get over it and go on to have a great birth and a beautiful baby and be a happy mother."

Yes, we chuckle. I almost did out loud—her words seem such a caricature of what we could dismiss as grandiose maternal expectations circa 2010. But pause to take a quick inventory of your emotional reactions? Is there empathy there, or more a mix of anxiety, annoy-ance, ridicule, anger? And on whose behalf: mother, or this child who will be born to this anxious mother and her expectations?

My guess is that, like me, you felt all of the above in the space of a few seconds, and your first concern was for the baby-to-be, for the consequences to this dyad of all this anxiety and grandiose expecta-tions not being met. I wondered what this woman would think if she knew this was my—our—reaction. Then I realized: She does know. She knows that we don't want to hear doubt and fear and lack of knowledge and the threat of unhappiness—and God knows what else—from a mother. Her unconscious knows that we will come for her hurling rocks if she shows us too much of herself.

She "knows" she should be serene, confident, happy, nondesiring, not anxious, that mothers cannot have subjectivity and all the desire that comes with that, because they are of paramount importance to the reproduction of citizens and consumers. Bad, desiring, feeling mothers make bad people who don't obey the rules and buy things and listen to their leaders and build our society into the Greatest Nation in the World. Even without having read the great theorists she knows she must be an unambivalent container, optimal responder, and sensi-tive nurturer, whose every emotion other than joy is suspect and has been written about, somewhere, as pathogenic.

The implication is that if she continues down this road of being persecuted by these floating objects, both internal and external, unwanted emotions may surface that could threaten the success of the entire project. She could have a difficult birth, an ugly, bad baby—or one that she feels is this way—and she could be an unhappy (read bad) mother. We all know that all of these things are not only possible, or even likely, but guaranteed. The birth will be difficult and painful—even a great birth is a monumental challenge and an uncanny, unset-tling experience—her baby will certainly not always be beautiful, and she will feel every emotion on the continuum from love to hate about this child and being a mother.

So what is this woman with her bad feelings coming on, floating into view like the return of the repressed, to do? She must obey this knowledge. She must try to banish her feelings and hide them at all costs. She may go to a counselor because that is allowed, but only if their project is to tamp all this down, to ensure the great, beautiful, happy result.

This is nothing like an uncomplicated birth for maternal subjectivity. This is nothing like the originary, idealized, eternally serene (and voiceless, powerless) Virgin Mary prototype—or perhaps she, too, had trouble being voiceless and forgotten up on her pedestal. I am asking how can a woman become a mother without hating herself on some level or cauterizing, erasing, splitting off major parts of herself, in the process?

My would-be patient is experiencing the beginning of becoming forced into a kind of paranoid subject position by maternity. She begins by thinking that her maternal drama is private—two blue lines on a stick in her bathroom—then she begins to fear that any failure, even in the delivery room, will represent a failure that seems to carry with it a shaming so severe as to cancel out her value as a person. So here any previous identity is subordinated to the incipient maternal identity—the maternal identity the woman hasn't even had a chance yet to form or call her own. She begins to be careful about what she lets on, because now she has begun to assume she is being watched, judged, and evaluated.

She doesn't yet know that what she knows—the voices in her head that tell her what she should feel, eat, do, think, want, and what she should not, as a mother—are not her voices but that they are hearsay, rumor, gossip, platitude, common knowledge, what goes without saying, the air we breathe—all the forces of discourse that prevent the emergence of dissenting voices. She doesn't yet know that she must embrace this paranoia. She must become suspicious, a reader between the lines, a decoder, a detective who bugs her own psyche, records her own words—how often do I call myself a "bad mother"—and a close textual reader who deconstructs the messages she gets from all those "helpful" people about what a mother is. This is the only way to become a mother who won't damn herself at every sign of her own existence. Perhaps we need to think there is no such thing as a mother, only a mother and the culture, until the mother develops a separate self.

It may be helpful to think of the emergent maternal subjectivity as a kind of emergent voice like the voice of subculture, nation, or people (in the case of, say, a postcolonial population) that must work to define itself apart from the constructions internalized from the colonial discourse. A centrally important part of becoming a mother is one's process of navigating this internal/external hailstorm during which one becomes a paranoid subject, visited by voices and narratives and injunctions. Becoming a mother happens simultaneously from without and within, like a hallucination. It is a part of the self that is more than a self-state. But what is it? How can we theorize it? We don't see it coming, and we don't see it once it's there. It is overdetermined, multiply sourced, unseen, spoken and unspoken. It is, in so many ways, parallel to the odd, uncanny experience of finding that another human being is growing inside your body.

If a certain basic level of becoming oriented doesn't happen, one becomes mad—and we should think about postpartum depression here.

The woman on the phone knew her problem was this intrusive symptom—the floaters in her eyes and the one in her womb—that was creating foreign feelings, or feelings that felt foreign, from some region of herself she did not want to recognize because it is not recognizable by the mother discourse. In this way, her floaters were a kind of doubling of the uncanny experience of becoming a mother. Not only does something begin to grow inside you, something that will get very large and start moving violently and then will want to come out a very small opening, but some new you begins to grow as well. You are not who you were, and you don't know yet what will come out but you know it should be good and beautiful and happy. Or else.

I think there's a whole dimension of the maternal experience that is unformulated and remains unintegrated, indescribable because we have not yet formulated the language, the grammar, as Suzanne Juhasz (2003) termed it, for the maternal experience. There is something odd, uncanny, unreal, almost supernatural about another person being made in one's body. Yet when we work with mothers, is this what we talk about? We assume the existence of and explore fantasies about everything else in a patient's life, yet of birth and motherhood there is so little written. Ruth Stein (Slavin, Oxenhandler, Seligman, Stein, & Davies, 2004) spoke about a thought that came into her head when she was in her first early days as a mother: "My son is a birthday cake which is being cut into pieces to eat" and about the "hyperreal clarity and luminosity" of it (p. 391). There have been some instances of what gets termed "maternal writing" here and there, but usually it is in a different typeface or in a margin, or set off by extra space within more academic, intellectual texts, which only reaffirms its unintegratable, uncanny, unformulated, primary process and therefore lesser status.

All of this leads me to Homi Bhabha (1994) and his writing on hybridity as a way to think beyond borders and designations of racial identity and essentialism to a place of unlimited potential and contingency in identity—and in the politics and activism that could follow from that. Mothers need this term. Having three children led me to understand that mothers—and the women who become them—become hybrids. I think there are many reasons that I had our third child, and one of them was a recombinant curiosity. With each child I've discovered a Venn diagram of self-states, overlapping and reforming and recombining, blending, bleeding into, deepening, recontouring each other, cross-fertilizing and cross-referencing each other, and I'm not sure I'm ever wholly in one state or in any state for long.

Some of the states are, according to the only words I have for them: The stay-at-home, full-time mother self, the desiring mother, the desiring mother who is ashamed of her desire, to love, to possess, to smother, to merge in love with, to touch, to be needed, wanted, thanked, possessed. The desiring mother who is ashamed at her desire to separate, to lose, to extricate, escape, injure, reject, give back. The nurturing mother, the person who watches herself being the nurturing mother and sees that she enjoys it, that she is sick of it, who hears her daughter say, "I'm lucky because I have a loves me mommy," and who feels badly for being very short with this child lately, for taking her away from the baby and the older one. The desiring to escape mother, the desiring to snuggle forever in the bosom of home mother, the being consumed mother (listening to my toddler gulp on my breast feels almost frightening—she's consuming me. I loved it once but now love it only when the new baby makes that sound. Floods me with calm. As it tapers off I become aware of a shift, anxious almost, wanting her to take more, wondering if she's had enough or thinks there's no more, should I switch her, will she get too much foremilk, should I contrive somehow to keep her here longer?). The mother who can remember myself before children, when I was only one. Within this ever-expanding hybridity of subjectivity, who can say anymore which state is pathogenic, good mother, good enough, or bad, separate or connected, too much or too little, consuming or consumed, full-time, or working?

The word *hybridity* originates from the Latin *hybrida*, which described the offspring of a tame sow and a wild boar. As such it is the perfect word for the meeting, within a woman, of the mother discourse and its opposite: the wild boar of her true spectrum of feelings and experience. And the culture's deep fear of a mother's complexity, and mistrust that she can integrate subjectivity and its accompanying registers of desire, while still preserving the ability to nurture, parallels fears of racial mixing and miscegenation, of hybrids as a diseased mutation, which of course are also part of the history of this term.

Right now my breasts are tingling as they fill with milk in anticipation of my baby's need. Apparently, they are thinking about her right now as I think about you. It has been several hours since I used the pump in my bag to drain the liquid my body has made, is always making, to prevent the human being that I felt move down inside me like a cinder block pushing through a tube, from dying. I've left her to be fed by another so that I can pursue this aspect of myself, the reflecting mother struggling out of the muteness of experience to know where I am.

The more I speak to mothers, the more I find deep shame at their maternal selves and mistrust in their own shifting states of subjectivity and desire. So far we have only staked out, as a culture, a set of binary positions for women who are mothers—good mother or bad, stay-at-home (read passive and merged) or working (read active, separate)—and everything they feel and do, when they come to review it in their heads or speak it in the world, ends up classified according to one or the other of these positions because that's all the language we have developed to describe our states. Even the "good enough mother" instinctively screws up only just the perfect optimal amount.

Mothers need to know that their experience is uncanny and that they must constantly both live their experience and siphon out the toxins through a process of talk and analysis and cultural critique that can be exhausting, without becoming so exhausted that they cannot mother. They must know that there are floaters and that there is no treatment for them. They must call counselors, and the counselors must know all this so they can tell the mothers.

BRINGING HISTORY TO MIND
Discussion of "Interpellations"

SUSIE ORBACH

In 1973 a group of fledgling psychotherapists—Luise Eichenbaum, Carol Bloom, Vicki Wurman, Laura Kogel, Lee Crespi, and myself— and one more experienced therapist, Lela Zaphiropoulos, set up a feminist therapist's study group. We had been drawn to a study of psychotherapy and increasingly psychoanalysis because we felt it could enhance our understanding of the construction of femininity, of class, of social markers such as race and ethnicity.

In approaching the chapters in this section of the book, that history—which I go on to detail—is brought to mind. These essays represent a later generation's endeavors to use psychoanalysis in not dissimilar ways, and in discussing them I veer between wondering whether the postmodern discourse that informs the essays integrates earlier work done on linking the personal subjective with the lived experience of masculinity and femininity or whether it ignores it. For this reason I bring that early work forward now to link in with the chapters in this section.

The group members were activists within the feminist movement and inheritors of the New Left tradition that saw, from the 1964 Port Huron statement on, the importance of the idea that the personal is political. But what did it really mean? We understood what it meant in political terms in the sense of trying to live one's lives according to one's beliefs. We understood that individual actions could be seen as a consequence of social positioning; we knew the political shaped the individual, but how exactly?

Consciousness raising, the basic tool of women's groups, had given us personal and sociological understandings of why we were the way we were up to a point. We understood why we did the nurturing and the housework, turned ourselves into objects of desire, deferred to others, felt guilty if we took up too much space, felt comforted by being able to care and help others initiate. And while consciousness raising was clearly a crucial, nay, revolutionary act, for us as individuals and for the whole Second Wave feminist surge, it left some of us especially interested in the details of how the lived experience of femininity, of becoming and feeling ourselves as women, operated at a psychic and intrapsychic level.

Psychotherapy and psychoanalysis are the disciplines that study the experience of the subject as well as the making of the subject. We, like the essayists, hastened to learn. To do our learning, we were eager to discover a methodology that would enable us to find out about the intricacies of psychic development, without simultaneously imbibing the psychoanalytic canon and its fixed ways of understanding human development within the Oedipal story. We wanted to learn how and in what ways one might begin to theorize the internalization of a feminized psychic structure as Sheehy tries to do: how exactly did the outside get inside (Eichenbaum & Orbach, 1982; Orbach, 1978) so that what felt right and "normal" were behaviors, emotions, ways of being that were, in the face of political analysis, seriously at odds with women's self-interest.

Franz Fanon had already published *Black Skin, White Masks* (1967) 20 years earlier, and there were precedents within psychoanalysis, particularly Wilhelm Reich's (1970, 1972, 1974) work and that of Karen Horney (1967), that encouraged us. It wasn't a popular move within feminism to turn to psychoanalysis,* as psychoanalysis had allowed itself to become a deeply reactionary practice in the post–World War II reinstating of women's role after the men returned from war. Then psychoanalysis found itself as ideological handmaiden proclaiming the true destiny and appropriate role for women—a role that was to explode with the publication of Friedan's *The Feminine Mystique* (1963), Greer's *The Female Eunuch* (1970), and countless other feminist writings.

Nevertheless, we were intrigued by psychoanalysis's capacity to reach those places not studied by any other discipline, so we set out to see what we might learn as we pursued the idea of deconstructing the terms of our own subordination.

---

* Juliet Mitchell was to publish *Psychoanalysis and Feminism* (1974) a year later.

There were of course similarities between therapy and the women's group that made it attractive. In both one speaks personally about the most private of experience with the aim of understanding. But whereas the women's group sought to make collective story out of the multiple testimony of individuals and to offer consolation and identification as the basis of a call to action, psychotherapy sought to find the particular.

Psychoanalysis is an in-depth study of the individual. From that psychoanalysis draws theory about psychological development and psychological imperatives. It was this purpose that emboldened us to feel that, using this approach, we might be able to more deeply understand, as do the essayists in this book the psychology of femininity.

So why all this history? I write it because of the need to welcome this project in the context of previous attempts to understand the intersection of the individual and society, of the social and the individual and of the ways we become human are intricately linked with how we become a human at a particular moment in history, in a particular family constellation with its psychology, class, ethnic, immigrant, educational, geographical situation. This is the implicit subject of the pieces in this collection; however, there is an interruption of these understandings, and the fact that generations lose what has gone before is no accident.

The loss arises in large measure as a consequence of the political project of the right, which would argue that there are science disciplines that are a-ideological. This is of course a preposterous nonsense. Just as any social science can be parsed from the neo-liberal to the Marxist to the postmodern,* whether that be economics or sociology, so too, the approaches to what constitutes the human subject are shaped by ideological perspective.

Let's take a simple example in our field. A common statement in clinical seminars† is that Jenny, a 35-year-old woman patient, is "needy." This shorthand description is a political as well as a psychological statement. Without context for what kind of needy and why

---

* For an interesting discussion of the use of ideology and economics, see Curtis (2004).
† This is common in the United Kingdom at very well-regarded therapy centers.

we would use that word to describe the ways she is, we are signaling something about prefeminist understandings of femininity. We are saying that the clinician in describing this woman in this manner is seeing her in limited terms or in terms that miss critical understandings of gendering. We are saying as much about the theory of the clinician as we are about the psychology of the woman.

The speaker is taking what may be an "is," without interrogation, and is unthinkingly reproducing popular magazine concepts of femininity. So let's try it again.

If we say that Jenny has hesitancy about expressing her desires, we are also making a politically inflected statement. The notion of hesitancy opens up a wedge between what is often an assumption about the psychology of women and allows us to think about the social forces that create this kind of a response in a woman's emotional life. If we add in a little more texture and say that she has a hesitancy about expressing her desires and thus presents in a way that shows disdain for herself, for the existence of her needs, for appearing insatiable, we are making a psychological and political statement for we are linking in our own minds the psychological disposition with the social impact of her upbringing.

If we think with yet more complexity and say that she has a hesitancy about expressing her desires and thus presents in a way that shows disdain for herself, for the existence of her needs, and, we add, her defense against exposing them is to present herself in such a way that she comes across—to herself and others—as insatiable, we are making a dynamic psychological statement as well as a political statement.

If we think through a gender-conscious lens, we see that she has a hesitancy about expressing her desires and thus presents in a way that shows disdain for herself, for the existence of her needs, and that she is reluctant to feel that what arises from her if it relates to her own needs rather than responding to the needs of others. We are using then well-worked-out feminist psychoanalytic theory to understand her. Feminist psychoanalytic theory (Chodorow, 1978; Eichenbaum & Orbach, 1982; Orbach, 1978) enables us to comprehend in broad terms the conflicted desire, the outward manifestation, the felt experience of the individual, and to some extent the impact on the other.

Such an approach implies ways of critiquing and questioning. It demonstrates how psychoanalytic thinking is always politically inflected. When we lose the capacity to question and instead take on the basic assumptions or perhaps the prejudices of the field in which we work—women are needy, women find it hard to separate—we are in an ideological vice.

For those of us who went on to form The Women's Therapy Centre* in London and The Women's Therapy Centre Institute† in New York City, we had to contest the basic psychoanalytic assumption that there was a human being onto which culture was overlaid. And in these essays, we see how this reformulated psychoanalytic practice has come through. These essays implicitly reject the notion of an a priori human being. They understand and work with the intrapsychic power of cultural imperative. The very strength and brilliance of the psychoanalytic endeavor is—at its best—to understand the ways in which x particular infant comes to be x particular adult. Or to put it more accurately, for we are talking now before infant observation and attachment theory became part of the psychoanalytic enterprise, to look retrospectively and surmise about the early childhood and infancy surrounds of x adult.

Without jettisoning the history, story, and myth making that have formed the Western subject over the 6,000 years but instead marrying it with the notion of the individual as a product of the particular culture one was raised in brought us our particular way of approaching psychoanalysis. That didn't mean we did culture instead of therapy in the consulting room, but it did mean that psychoanalysis could help us see the ways the cultural familial setting took the set of possibilities that constitutes the human infant and enables that infant, and subsequently the child, to develop in their idiosyncratic and deeply personal ways.

This approach to our psychoanalytic studies meant that we would not elevate the understanding above others (e.g., economics, anthropology, feminism). Guralnik, of course, carries this tradition forward in her approach to Raven. Like us she uses aspects of psychoanalysis,

---

* An outpatient center serving women and their families since 1976 now in receipt of local and national government funding and offering psychotherapy to women in many different languages.
† A small training organization based on feminist principles and offering postgraduate training from a gender-conscious perspective.

rather than psychoanalysis becoming the only means to approach an understanding of Raven.

An enriched psychoanalysis can enable theory building on the construction of femininity and the process of woman-to-woman therapy. Crucial to this has been psychoanalysis' conception of unconscious processes, of transference, and of countertransference. Equally important were learnings from women's consciousness-raising groups, namely, issues of personal identification with the individual and of the social role of women and the psychological pressures that created.

We started from the following assumption: if women are to feel more or less in tune with a set of beliefs and practices about their individual place in the world and the possibilities that exist for them, if late 20th-century forms of femininity have individual salience, then what are the psychic mechanisms in play that make that possible? And if it is possible for the women we see in therapy, what and how do those mechanisms work inside of us? What do we understand about the struggles of our patients; what do we understand about, for example, their hesitancy and disdain about their own needs, based on our personal experience of curbing and disdaining our own? Without imposing our own story and comprehension on the other, what is there that we can interpolate from our experience?

This approach to our work became codified in our work at The Women's Therapy Centre in London where a five-step peer supervision model began with the therapist's description of the person she was working with, including details of her family of origin, her class and ethnic background, her current situation, her sexual orientation, her presenting problems on entering therapy, and the course of her therapy up to that point (see Eichenbaum & Orbach, 1982, p. 135). In step two the therapists share their identification with the person being discussed, noting any points that resemble their own life and being aware of when during the presentation they were particularly moved. Step three moved on to the specifics of gender and how the woman's distress might be understood. We were particularly keen to notice where the presenting problem or distress related to her struggle to be an adult woman. Step four was more technical in the sense of distinguishing among countertransference, identification, the therapist's transference, and mother–daughter dynamics. Step five was follow-up in a month.

It occurred to me as I was reading the chapters in this section of the ways one has to insist once again on the legitimacy of the attempt to understand people in their context. These chapters illustrate that neither analyst nor analysand can be extracted from an understanding of his or her background yet be made sense of in any useful way. Background creates foreground in unique ways and to understand, to be helpful, is to remember our own intellectual and psychological history and social circumstances.

Guralnik's discussion of the schoolgirl Raven, the circumstances of her milieu—biracial, with parents detached from their backgrounds—shows us the necessity of understanding the contemporary cultural story that presses on the young woman's attempt to create an identity. It is a story about the significance of the body today. It is a story about race and place. It is a story about sexual markers. As in anorexia, body modification, body hooking, and scarring are the contemporary ways "the body is used to transcend the body." In Raven's toleration of the self-inflicted pain, she finds herself alive. Defying the binaries of girl–boy, straight–gay, and Black–White and the cultural propensity to think one understands the other by reference to the baldness of category, body modification becomes a way to make a new body, a body that cannot be claimed by others, a body in the process of self-definition. The body, the site of the most intense attention by commercial forces that have done much to destabilize it, becomes in the hands of Raven, her identity. By not disturbing that idea but meeting it, Guralnik turns acts that might otherwise appear offensive or self-destructive into moments of connection. Guralnik is not frightened by the body practice, presumably finding within herself points of identification in the search for a body.

In this account of the work, one gets the sense that, because the details of Raven's background are spectacular, it is assumed that they are understood. I wondered whether their meaning for Raven could use further unpacking. Without that, "Reality" comes from flesh cut into. That is the materiality of her existence. The body today, just as the psyche, is an intersubjective construction. The body is not symptom but a body in the making (Orbach, 2009). The conundrum lays in the fact that language—talking, explaining, asking—is not the idiom of this family, and the therapy itself enacts this hesitation.

In Hartman's discussion I am brought up short almost from the beginning. He talks of mapping the political zones as a way back into the psychodynamics. I am sympathetic to that approach but confused. How does a political understanding of gender not come into view with someone? We are all gendered, and we all create in others a sense of our gender. We know that the internal experience of gender may differ from its external representation; it may be more fluid, more troubled, or indeed more fixed and that the internalization of gender speaks to social norms and constraints. So that is not my confusion. What does confuse me is the representation of need and homosexuality as weakness. Both Mother's fear of her own need and Darren's fear of disturbing the familial order by expressing his love for a man are represented as weakness. Notions of masculinity as strength and femininity as neediness replete with notions of the mother as castrating throw me. Are these categories being critiqued or accepted? I believe both, and that there is an ironic touch to Hartman's use of these categories.

For in Dominic we have a representation of masculinity and sexuality that defies the stereotypes and allows Darren to be "brought more fully into being." The internalized self-hatred that is in Darren is allowed to soften. But I have questions about Hartman's use of the terms *masculine* and *feminine* roles. I am not sure what he means by these. Are these fixed or desirable categories? Are these emotional categories? Are these about permission and restriction?

A contribution of feminism was to insist that what a woman does is "feminine." It is not masculinity that allows her to differentiate or be forceful but that she is expanding the internal notions and psychic possibilities of femininity. When she does something at odds with the designated gender category, she is not degendering herself but rather extending the possibilities of experience. Without losing the power of the concepts of feminized and masculinized, particularly as defense structures, we must still interrogate them and notice when we wish to present our understandings of the transference–countertransference dynamics within these terms. What is it that we are really grasping for? Are these terms of critique? Are these shorthand? Or are they unexamined conceptions that require addressing? It is clear that Darren has gained much from the therapy, as has Hartman. I have a sense though that the political lens could be brought to the language in general, opening up the tendencies we all share to classify rather than explore what we are trying to reveal.

In Lobban's chapter, the discovery of "coloured blood" in post-Apartheid South Africa presages a most profound journey into the racialized self. The therapist discovers that all is not as she thought, and in her renegotiation with the terms of her social position her psychological sense of self dissolves. Ingeniously, as she goes through her journey of reencountering the terms of her engagement with self and the wider world, she takes herself as patient and, for the reader at least, dissects the processes by which she comes upon shock, sorrow, abjection, and acceptance.

In Lobban's taking of the DNA test we see how fragile is the sense of Whiteness. Legally enshrined until 1993, apartheid structures the relations of all, whatever their racial designation, and this is the strength of Lobban's chapter. From her first excitement at discovering she had blood in common with the people whose justice she was fighting for through to the destabilization of self and sense of loss and confusion of an identity she had inhabited, we see the impact of state powerlessness and oppression created in the individual. By continually taking herself as a subject for analysis, she allows us to see the complex and deeply personal ways racism marks us. The divide between White and Coloured is huge, but the impact of Whiteness is shown to be a category far less stable than previously imagined.

In seminars on social class that Luise Eichenbaum and I ran* in that most class-conscious of societies—Britain—we saw something similar yet not so brave. In asking women therapists to engage with their personal class position and then background and then the class position of their grandparents and background of their relatives, we came upon a large number of women who were either first- or second-generation middle class and educated. In a way that discovery was not surprising for this was the post–World War II generation for whom education was being opened up. In another way it was surprising as

---

* At The Women's Therapy Centre in London in 1979.

all these women projected a sense of solidity within their middle-class identities—so strongly in fact, that they did not recognize the impact of their class position as read through accent and attitude on their patients. Indeed the very reason we had initiated seminars on class was because class issues did not seem to arise with the patients of British therapists, whereas the hurt associated with class came up in sessions with therapists whose North American or South African intonation or accent was obvious.

The "discovery" of a working class background chimes with similar delight to Lobban's on her first discovering she was part "Coloured." In British society there was so much at stake about class that the therapists at the center needed to create the conditions for exploring the intrapsychic impact of it as Lobban so brilliantly does with herself.

All these chapters are engaged in a conversation with each other, and Rozmarin addresses this in his insistence that language, intervention, thinking, and speaking are not neutral. For me, and Rozmarin I believe, the meaning of words is created with reference to their context and in the psychoanalytic context this will involve the shared space as well as the separate spaces the analyst and analysand occupy. The ideals of psychoanalysis are for neutrality, but this of course is an idealist notion. Neutrality is a goal, not a given. Every comment that the analyst makes is inflected by her or his theoretical stance. We don't just ask any question or offer any commentary; we ask specific questions that reflect our personal interests, and we offer commentary based on our understandings. Our own training analysis and supervision are there to enable us to think beyond the things we find difficult in our patient's material. We encounter emotional tableaus, moral dilemmas, sexual and personal practices that may be deeply at odds with our own codes, and to be of use to the individual we have to explore our own reactions and unpick our prejudices.

We learn to be curious in relation to our responses: I wonder why I feel this; I wonder why this makes me uneasy; I wonder what this is touching on for me and so on. In this way we develop a curiosity toward our own responses that becomes part of the way we then engage with our patients.

Rozmarin's point about the way he felt constrained to question Jonathan's hurry showed considerable sensitivity to the continuing discrimination that haunts us as a culture around homosexual love. But I wonder whether in his wish to support his patient and follow his cues he doesn't inadvertently foreclose the very issues he would wish to pose by being reluctant to bring that into the room in a way that would acknowledge his hesitancy. When a patient is über-certain himself, recognizing with tact his certainty in a comment that goes behind and underneath what he is clinging to can then lead to a more questioning. To not speak is not a neutral endeavor, as is speaking. They are both loaded with meaning that is suffused with social and psychological signifiers.

Pugachevsky's chapter moves us into two subjects that appear to be open in our society but as revealed in Amy's experience are far from it: the Holocaust and sexuality. The former is so normalized in Amy's experience that it doesn't emerge in the therapy until the therapist prompts it. The therapist doesn't prompt until she goes to supervision because she herself has the same third-generation Holocaust designate mourner position in her family and had walled off the awareness and thus the identification in the session. It is not reductionist to say that patterns of experience emerge that are the outcome of history. The supervisor asks "Jewish" and then says "Holocaust" because he senses a whole set of responses that arise in the subsequent generations. His intervention allows analyst and analysand to speak. They talk about the Holocaust and the horrors of what they have carried, and the presenting problem dissolves. In its dissolution, so too dissolves the therapy, not, one suspects, the internal relationship, because it has so transformed Amy, but the actuality of her coming to therapy.

This is a beautiful chapter about the sensitive engagement with a woman whose cautiousness has made her a "bit high-strung, a bit of a neat freak, a bit of a health nut" and who viewed corporeality as fragile. By being unafraid to discuss the body and what happens in sexual arousal, Pugachevsky demonstrates the possibility that there are pleasures with being "out of control." Orgasm and sexual excitement are—in contrast to how physical risks are addressed by her parents—pleasurable. This notion that the body can surrender without being endangered is the gift that Pugachevsky gives to Amy. That Amy leaves can be seen as her keeping a new secret, her secret and not the family legacy.

All analysts have to draw upon their own story and knowledges to discuss the historical situation of their patient's family. We aren't all third-generation Holocaust mourners; we aren't all new immigrants; we aren't all WASPS; we aren't all gay; we aren't all Irish working class; we aren't all Mexican or Vietnamese or Serbian. Categories that get flagged up in therapy are portals for investigation. By being inquisitive we learn about the experience of the other, the feel of their mental and physical life within their family and the ways that family was or was not embedded in the culture.

In encountering Sheehy's fine chapter, I am reminded how very British I am. I notice in my North American patients and when I visit the commandment for things to be great. Her patient wants to have a great birth—and as if that is not enough, a beautiful baby and be a happy mother. My response is to cringe inside. Why great? Why beautiful? Why happy? Why the superlatives? What is going on in the United States that I can't go into a store to look at a pair of shoes or buy a newspaper without being admonished to have a peak experience? I don't dislike overstatement, but I do abhor the synthetic nature of happiness founded on great. Emotional literacy, poetry, literature, art, living, show us that the thing we call happiness is a result of being able to metabolize a range of emotions from the grand, the inspirational and dramatic ones to the more subtle. Think where happiness would flounder if we couldn't feel dismay. As Sheehy's chapter shows this is contemporary mothering: It has to be perfect, yet as we know it is a process—messy and wonderful and difficult and moving and disturbing and sexy and insecure making. It is all of these things and more.

The baby arrives and makes the woman into a mother, and in contemporary discourse the requirements on this mother are endless. There is no way for her to meet them because mother-becoming is not paint by numbers. Mother-becoming is a painful, exhilarating, exhausting, confusing, calming, physical-psychological conversation with a self that is developing as it enables the new life of the baby to unfold. And it is a conversation that is deeply cultural as Sheehy shows. Her potential patient is becoming a North American, New York mother, with all that this demands. She can arm her with knowledge of the madness of expectation and what is coming. She can empathize with her. She can change the nature of what it means to "have a great birth and a beautiful baby and be a happy mother." This is what a culturally savvy, politically informed, critical psychotherapist–mother can offer and it is certainly worth having. She can help "fit" her patient to sit inside herself and take a space from the cultural pressures that besiege even as she negotiates them.

Addressing cultural familial intrapsychic and interpsychic pressures is what we do. As we try to create connection and understanding we discover, too, where we and the analysand cannot connect and be understood. It is in those blanks as much as in the points of identification and comprehension that psychoanalysis does its work. Our humility in acknowledging what we can't know, what we can't reach, what is outside, is as critical as where we can know and reach. Our effort is always to enter the mental space of the other, in its fullest dimensions. Therapy doesn't change the world; it allows us to live in it differently.

PART III

SUBJECTIVE EXPERIENCE, COLLECTIVE NARRATIVES

13

INTERPELLATING GRACE

ORNA GURALNIK

EDITOR'S INTRODUCTION

The meeting of psyche and society is particularly intense and rich at the site of sexuality. Working "the seam between the self and the world" that constitutes psychoanalysis, Guralnik employs concepts from psychoanalysis and cultural theory that sit right on that seam. Addressing the depersonalization suffered by her patient Grace, who is a lesbian, she probes the nexus of interpellation and intelligibility. She shows how the gratifying recognition fostered by these processes also entails misrecognition, even erasure, and shame. Here Guralnik tells us the astonishing story of how Grace's heterosexual friends try to make her intelligible by trying to preserve heterosexuality at the expense of monogamy.

Recently, my patient Grace relayed the following incident: She and her girlfriend Lila were at their neighborhood dive bar where they met with their straight drinking buddies, Joan and Joe. After years of analysis Grace was becoming comfortable with herself and playfully asked her buddies if they knew she and Lila were gay. Friends met play with play: "Duh. Of course we knew!" Grace pushed on, sharing that they were thinking of having a baby. Giddy and excited, the group erupted into a surprising turn of conversation.

Joan was offering Joe up for sperm donation.

Ooh-ahhh—Grace and Lila exclaimed how attractive Joe indeed was but coyly declined. Joan insisted. Grace and Lila refused. At some point in the evening Grace found herself momentarily alone with Joe. He cornered her and tried to come on to her, confessing how turned on he was by her and moving alarmingly close. Grace wriggled away, and soon after she and Lila left.

123

Grace arrived to her next session in a mixed state; in a giddy combo of flattered yet befuddled, she relayed the story. She was both closer and further away from having a baby than ever. She was shifty but could not tell what was stirring her; her *excitement* was increasingly muffled by the old smog of depersonalization. Crowding in, stealing her experience.

Depersonalization, a condition that plagued Grace since her early teens, is the subjective experience of profound estrangement, an altered state of consciousness that is often described as feeling numb, like a robot, lacking feelings or physical sensations. People witness their lives "from the ceiling," as if it were a movie. It can hit like a clap of thunder, become chronic, or come and go in response to triggers. It is a form of dissociation, which nowadays we understand as the psyche's fragmentation in response to the unbearable. I have come to think of depersonalization and dissociative fragmentation as a mirror of how discourse has shaped, and shaved, the subject and her desire. By *discourse* here I mean the culturally shared implicit constraints on what can be spoken of. And by *subjectivity* I am not referring to the given essential subject but to the poststructural subject constituted within these constraints, the constraints that sanction certain ways of being normative and intelligible while foreclosing others.

Seems elemental: Grace grew up in a Christian world where people are straight and girls are not sexual. From this perspective, her parents are not only her attachment objects, to be internalized, incorporated, or introjected to populate her internal world but are also *agents*, passing on normative regulations. As an adolescent, Grace's young mind was busy trying to fend off the strange urges her body was sending her. Puberty. Urges like doodles of an incomprehensible nature. *Après coup*, we can guess that girls girls girls were on the gates of her mind. She attempted to tame these urges by inviting her mother for long walks and talks, in which she would endlessly confess, begging forgiveness for any stray thought she might have had: petty theft, jealousy, masturbation. No matter how reassuring mother was, no confession hit the spot. Grace just could not find a way to format these urges in a way she could live with. Tormented, she often gave up her attempts to "fix it" and spent long stretches in the bathroom, holding her breath till she "saw stars" or fixing her gaze in the mirror till it "all went quiet." She was teaching herself to dissociate, away from the *shame of unintelligibility*—the *"escape when there is no escape"* (Putnam's classic).

A bit more theory: To be psychically born into the social order, one needs to *invite* recognition from the world. Jessica Benjamin (1988) describes how a person comes to feel like "the doer who does, the author of my acts" (p. 21), by being with another person who recognizes her. In Bakhtin's words (1984, p. 287), "I am conscious of myself and become myself only while revealing myself to another.... A person has no sovereign territory; he is always on the boundary; looking inside himself, he looks into the eyes of another or with the eyes of another."

Recognition is the life-giving exchange with others.

To become a citizen of society, to share meaning with others, one needs to articulate oneself in the language of one's time and place, in discourse, not only to one's "objects." To become a subject with power and agency, one needs to invite the world in to constitute one's subjectivity. This desire-to-be-a-subject is also the site for regulatory power to take hold. Thus, often, recognition arrives in the form of a branding machine, coming at the raw and unformulated to give it shape—language, history, social order all folded into the structure of discourse. And the ideology it circulates.

Althusser's (2001) work on *interpellation* has had a particularly profound impact on my theoretical and clinical psychoanalytic work. (This has much to do with my choice to live away from my possessive homeland of Israel. Good ideology presents itself as if it is the natural order of things. It is only when you depart can you see the water you swam in.) Althusser elaborated on the concept of interpellation to describe the very mechanism through which ideology takes hold of the subject, calls the individual into a particular way of being. Ideology, the collective's unconscious beliefs and secrets that instruct us what the good life is is what unites us as obedient and productive citizens (Foucault, 1988–1990). Ideology stands outside the individual, calling on it. This site within the subject that I am referring to is where ideology lodges itself, tying us to the various State Apparatuses (e.g., the military or the Social Security Administration).

A patient of Jacques Lacan, Althusser was inspired by psychoanalysis and structuralism to investigate *how the voice of the State calls us into social existence.* "HEY YOU!" hails the police officer—and we each turn a guilty turn to face our master: *What did I do?* There is a place in us, ready to receive this call from the state. In turning, an unconscious, *implicit* drama had already occurred in us, revealed when we know it is US the police officer is calling, or it is *you* that is the object of a cat-call, or the stare of the homeless asking for a quarter. "Yes, of course, it is singular *me* you recognized!" Nor must another absolute subject be present for a moment in which you are called to identify yourself and you turn: see the Israeli siren on memorial days, or the National Anthem—stand up, bow your head! We find a consolingly coherent image of our self reflected back in the "mirror" of dominant ideological discourse, a self-state that renders many other subject positions forsaken.

Depersonalization is particularly revealing of how the very instructions that constitute us as subjects can also paradoxically be responsible for our psychic fragmentation. The *space between recognition and interpellation* is where one's personhood and de-personhood are repeatedly carved out.

From this perspective, Grace's mom and family are not separate from their church and era—all blind to a desire she has no way to comprehend herself, which lays there, abject. Caught, she alternated between banging on the door—*"Let me in, mother of all hegemonies,"* harassing her mom with her excitement and petty crimes, asking to be interpellated—and giving up, numb and defeated, depersonalized. Trying to find herself in a maternal mind of course later repeated itself in her analysis with me—a chance to revisit interpellative injunctions.

***

How does this awareness affect my work as an analyst?

The moment in which her straight male friend came on to her, offering his sperm, was highly charged and seductive to Grace. In telling me about the incident she was all radar: Where will I place myself? *What subject position will my gaze ask her to take?* Was this the sign we've been waiting for? Could she unload her lesbian burden and have a child with a man? A part of her was craving an interpretation that would anchor her in the prevailing hegemony, a sign that she could terminate her exile. If I were to work from the inside out, aiming toward the object-related and interpersonal material packed in that moment, I believe I would have missed a chance to track the forcefulness of interpellation at work in this episode. I moved toward an interpretation saturated with the theory I am espousing here: not her feelings right this minute. My empathic resonance with her feeling state is informed by what I believe shapes these affect states. I am interested in analyzing what happened "out there" that ends up messing her up "in here." In coming out to a straight world, claiming the desire and entitlement *to have what others do—a child of their own*, Grace and Lila are sending shockwaves into the social order. They are to be boxed back in.

At this time in her analysis there occurred a remark widely attributed to President George W. Bush, an absolute subject: "The homosexuals getting married leave the people [emphasis added] with no recourse." There are people, and there are homosexuals.

And a snippet from our conversation:

G: Maybe I'm straight after all?

Me: It's good to feel embraced by the straight world, isn't it? You feel warm and calm.

G: He was really coming on to me. Why am I ashamed?

Me: I think he couldn't stand losing you to your gayness. He is offering you some way back from the lonely exile of being a lesbian.

With interpellation in mind, I read Joe as speaking to Grace, hailing her, from the locale of a heterosexual man "I know who you are. Respond to my/our calling: Hey you woman, I want you." And more: "You can/you will have my baby." Joe and Joan were destabilized by the possibility of a lesbian mother. They retaliated with their desire to straighten out the situation. This move was stronger than their lover's bond of monogamy and exclusivity. Joan: *Here, you can have my lover's sperm.* What is their relationship compared with the importance of converting back these lost souls?

Think: the un-thinkability of homosexual love. Ideology homogenizes the world. Lesbian Maternality is beyond the boundaries of intelligibility.

The immediate effect of such interpretations was to blow the thick smog of shame from the very internal toward the conflicted transitional space where Grace's subjectivity and her social context were dancing. Ultimately, these interventions were at the heart of her slow emergence out of depersonalization.

Depersonalization is an example of intelligibility's price tag. What is a livable life? In this clinical vignette and political arena, violence was waged against my patient by exclusion from representation, or more precisely, by the offer made to her for a place in discourse that ordains on the one yet continues to foreclose on the other. In some ways this is the worst kind of attack; as Butler (2004) says, "To be prohibited explicitly is to occupy a discursive site from which something like a reverse-discourse can be articulated" (p. 127). Living outside the norm places one at risk of death, sometimes actual death, but more frequently the social death of delegitimization and nonrecognition.

In our offices we try to crack open new conditions of possibility.

14

DARREN THEN HARVEY

The Incest Taboo Reconsidered, the Collective Unconscious Reprised

STEPHEN HARTMAN

EDITOR'S INTRODUCTION

Here Hartman riffs on the notion of the collective unconscious. Writing of his patient Darren, whose session immediately precedes that of Harvey, Hartman proposes we think in terms of collective affect, for example, anxiety, which we might further think in terms of recursivity, an idea Edgar Levenson (1983) has deployed to great clinical use. Considering the transference–countertransference schemas ignited by his patients' sexual practices, he takes up several concepts valuable for thinking about sex in clinical situations: erotic identification in undifferentiated states, the incest taboo as policing collective erotic identification, and the psychoanalytic insistence on libidinal hotbeds.

In this chapter, I wrestle with a lapse in my capacity to think or speak about an aspect of my patients' experience that felt threatening to me. I move from querying my aversive personal reaction to the drug and sex practices of three patients (specifically, their use of crystal meth and "barebacking"—unprotected anal sex with potentially HIV-positive partners) to questioning how taboo topics help us map the infiltration of social discourse in zones of unconscious "personal" discomfort. Once again, I am grateful to Darren (see Chapters 2 and 8) for helping me find my way there.

I hope to demonstrate that anxieties that may seem to comprise *my* countertransference, anxieties that appear to be part of one's unique psychic makeup, may have a more collective origin. Such collective anxieties may not be any better metabolized or *related* than schizoid anxieties. Discrimination, for instance, can be just as "unconscious" as self-hatred with the effect of disguising the recursive, mutually reinforcing relation between the two.

So it is that, in each story of barebacking that I will describe, I catch myself in a "wild" state of angst, dutifully fending off an eminent psychic retreat and restraining an instinct to protect a member of my tribe. In the process, I catch the two impulses in *psychic/social* bed. I observe that my anxiety about barebacking regurgitates normative homophobic messages and that I gird to expel *my* anxiety by going inward with personal recriminations. By folding in, I isolate myself from my anxiety yet also from finding containment in a nascent collective *eros*. My point is that in this attack on linking psychic retreats with collective solutions, we can trace a paradoxical feature of the incest taboo: An attack on a collective, libidinal register (the romance of families) is disguised by deference to an individual's traumatizing family romance. By the time *I got all my sisters with me*, we ain't family anymore.

Not so long ago, when I was a beginning candidate in psychoanalytic training, a very clever man contacted me about treatment. I was looking for an analytic case. He wanted treatment. Harvey was articulate, funny, and, not unbeknownst to him, a mess. His promising career as a sitcom writer was in shambles thanks to a lethal cocktail of envy, masochism, and crystal meth.

At the time, I considered it my duty as a gay man to fight the scourge of methamphetamine that was afflicting my community. When I look back, my attitude was anything but "analytic": I had a zero-tolerance policy with meth and no sympathy for crystal users. Were I not so green and in need of billable hours, I wonder if I would have agreed to treat people who needed to share an experience that I found unspeakable and that I was unwilling to imagine? The addictions roller-coaster ride is one problem; then there is the incessant, greedy sex talk that rarely reaches beyond recitation of who fucked whom. Listening to it, over and over again, feels deadening if not infectious. How many details of unbridled debauchery does the good doctor listen to before fantasizing what it would be like to check out a barebacking party? "No way! Not me!" I shrink viscerally from any incipient identification with quote-unquote *uninhibited*, self-declared *sex pigs.* "Countertransference intolerance?" I ask myself? "No," I answer, "just sanity." "Prudishness about orgiastic erotics?" "No," I reassure myself, "just respect for the individual." In any case, I took an immediate liking to Harvey in whose personal history I saw elements of my own story gone seriously awry.

Before contacting me, Harvey had petitioned at a conservative institute to be a control case. He interviewed with a kind, fatherly looking physician who spoke little and didn't inquire about Harvey's substance use. He did perk up when Harvey inched toward his sex life. Vaudevillian by nature, Harvey launched into a witty tale of sexual daring-do that only he could tell. There was the ventriloquist who could make your dick talk while he blew you, the Zen Master who looked like Tarzan but sounded more like Jane, the contortionist who twisted like a pretzel to make Harvey suck him off while chewing on his feet, and the self-described *"party and play* cum dumpster" whose penchant for sexual self-destruction seemed even more insatiable than Harvey's own. "You've had how many lovers?" the stern, fatherly acting doctor asked. Naively, and smitten by his bodacious performance, Harvey replied, "You mean, this month or this week?" "*Oy vey!*" the doctor groaned, showing Harvey to the door. "So much for the basic rule," was Harvey's parting salvo. "Some things can't be talked about." Harvey fled the office and high-tailed it to the baths.

Some things we analysts don't like to mention either—like when our libidinal needs outside of the session blur with our patients' own. It's a small town, the gay analytic world. Patients have seen me off the clock. I don't hide, nor do I seek opportunities to flaunt being only human. Still, I recall getting a phone call recently from a patient whom I treated a few years ago. Glen had seen me dancing shirtless at a circuit party back in the day. He had written me a letter that he wanted to send me. I shuddered, imagining that Glen was going to take me to task for preaching individual responsibility in the office while reveling in the charivari after hours. Had I given my blessing to the untoward and self-destructive impulses that my patient of strict Calvinist parents struggled not to renounce? Would he blame me for some variety of addiction? Wasn't I supposed to model decorum and decency and law-abiding, even if self-effacing, deferral of libidinal PDA? Suffice it to say that I had tried to talk about our interaction back then. He explained how debased he felt in the pleasure dome. It was all the more pathetic to find me among the crowd. What was I to say: that for me it was just silly fun? Or, maybe, that for me it was a way to reconnoiter with an early primal scene: woozy in the chlorinated collective that was the changing room on the occasion of my first swimming lesson? It seemed impossible not to make *his* problem *our* problem and *our* problem not about me. Anyway, by then, he had moved on to another therapist.

Defensively, my thoughts turned to Darren and other patients whose experience I could command to shore up my rationale for going public with pleasure. Darren was shy about displaying his very sculpted body in public at the time, though this would not have been readily apparent to the many who ogled him. He was starved for recognition of his physical presence among other men. Yet Darren felt ashamed of this need and, somehow, rather afraid at parties where men strutted their stuff and blended into one another in more or less equal measure. Darren would speak at length in sessions of his hope that I would be present at the big gay clubs. If I were, and from time to time I was, Darren would stand at the top of the stairs searching for me in the crowd. We would lock a gaze, nod, and Darren would come to life reigning over the staircase as the prodigal son of his go-go boy therapist.

However triumphant the night, the afterglow felt incesty to Darren and to me too. We wonder about it together. Darren describes his father, queasy with pleasure, at the sight of his wrestler son in his tight singlet. Darren couldn't parse his father's shame at the homoerotic scene from his own. This snapshot of melancholic gender, as Butler (1995) aptly named it, became Darren's fetish. Every trip to the gym, most trips to my office, and too many adventures with a trick were staged to recapture the awkward moment when father and son would disavow holding in mind the other's unseemly desire.

So much for transference. The shit hit the fan when Darren cautiously told me one day about his fantasies of barebacking. He had been with a man who insisted on being fucked without a condom. Darren said no but conceded that he had engaged in some preliminary unprotected play. I felt panic. I remember thinking, "Not Darren; not on my watch," as if I were solely responsible for Darren's sero-integrity. I dropped my guard and prematurely shot my wad: "You can't do that!" I explained. Deflated, Darren started to cry.

On reflection, in my state of high anxiety, I had made two egregious errors, albeit out of concern. I refused us, Darren and me, any kind of reciprocal identification that would have held and contextualized the nascent fantasy so that its meaning, and particularly its social aspect, could be explored. Then, I raped him—forced the Law of the Father right up his ass. We were both horrified.

My refusal to think about barebacking reflects three impulses that, I believe, are prevalent in psychoanalysis despite our best intentions to be open to whatever comes. First, as Dimen and Goldner (2005) stated eloquently, there is tremendous, often unconscious anxiety that mounts when we are prompted to think about sex: Eew! Consider group sex among nonpaired, potentially lethal partners: Bedlam! Second, we have yet to fully elaborate a theory of unconscious identification that registers at the social level. Might there be something psychically important (some form of care) that happens in the collective imagining of a scene that, when pared down to the individual, seems too lethal to consider? And, third, as I have argued elsewhere (Hartman, 2010), we have no scheme for "interembodiment" to match our zeal for intersubjectivity. Combine these ingredients, and we see anxiety mount with the rapid thrust of the incest taboo.

When Freud described the incest taboo and later paired it with Oedipal gymnastics, he had in mind a 1:1 ratio of sexual identification. He considered it evolutionarily sound for the Western neurotic to repress the instinct toward promiscuous discharge of libido in favor of *genital love* and *aim-inhibited love*. "Genital love," he wrote, "leads to the formation of new families, and aim-inhibited love to 'friendships' which become valuable from a cultural standpoint because they escape some of the limitations of genital love, as, for instance, its exclusiveness" (1930/1961, p. 50). When one identifies (or disidentifies) with one erotic object at a time, the matrix of social relationships is "regulated" and "civilized." Any need to discharge a collective erotic aim is sublimated into something like sportsmanship ("Eew!" happens to one person at a time) so that it becomes difficult for us to imagine what identification at the social-erotic level might be even while we root for the same team.*

Here I am indebted to Francisco Gonzalez (2009), who points out that erotic identification in undifferentiated states was never considered a viable alternative to the algorithm that one father plus one mother yields the requisite struggle for superego development. Freud viewed "exclusiveness" as a necessary sacrifice. By imposing order on the basic family unit, its effects reverberated in the social structure, "for there would be no prospect of curbing the sexual lusts of adults if the ground had not been prepared for it in childhood" (p. 51). Identification in the social realm was too lawless, too perverse, and too aligned with primitive states to be configured in the evolution of the psyche. The polygamous aim, once connected to the (singular) object, was not free to float except in the weigh station of the transference where it would, sooner or later, settle on an appropriate object. This wasn't altogether fair, Freud noted; indeed, he called it the source of "serious injustice" to individuals whose psychic constitution was not heterosexual and for whom the sexual aim may not be bound to a singular object. But it ensured, in normal folk, that "the whole of their sexual interests would flow without loss into the channels that are left open" (p. 52)—in other words reproduction and society.

The incest taboo thus functions to restrain us from lawless desire. It polices collective erotic identification and anything that we might more generally call a "collective unconscious." It decrees that, should psychoanalysts after Freud theorize erotic identification in social milieus, they do so at their own peril. Indeed, it may at first seem difficult to imagine what a social erotic aim or identification would look like because psychoanalysis has generally regarded sex in the bushes, among multiple strangers, on drugs, and in the fog of polymorphous body parts as perverse. When the sexual objects of the analyst and the analysand foray into a communal zone, where objects mix and identification is social, the incest taboo demands that each analyst shoulder his own countertransference. Psychoanalytic institutes become

---

* See Butler (1990) for a detailed account of the role of sublimation and the collapse of the collective in Freud and Marcuse's writing on the incest taboo.

hotbeds of controversy—called upon, much like me with Darren, to protect the innocent and yet contain our collective *imaginaire*.

When Darren left my office, Harvey walked in. Some days have a theme, and this was one. Harvey nervously tells me that he picked up. He found himself at a sex party. There was a feeble attempt to distribute condoms but, as the evening became morning, none were in use. Harvey, who is HIV negative and who walks a fine line between bravado and shame, was in awe. In the blending of bodies, and in the fog of omnipotence that enveloped him, he felt free, for once, of seeing himself the odd man out. As he described something more like blending than pairing, I grew hyperalert yet felt altogether depleted. My thoughts were very concrete. "He didn't! Oh my God," I found myself bracing against terror, worried about his sero-status, and Darren's, and mine. I became, in Gerson's terms (2009, p. 3), "a dead third."

Fresh from my mistake with Darren, I decided to ride it out. I fight the impulse to rush in with a safe-sex lesson. As Harvey continues to describe a scene that I dare not allow myself to imagine, I become aroused. I feel dirty, incestuous. I feel that this moment is unspeakable. There is nothing to do but let fear sweep through me and await the vice squad's arrival to single me out as traitor and pervert.

Harvey notices a shift in my affect. He makes a comment that I often use in similar moments: "You just took a little trip." I am struck that he borrows an idiom that I have often used to inquire about his dissociated travels (and, at that, an idiom that I inherited from my own analyst). Something about the turn to shared language in a moment of affective meltdown is free of the usual complementarity. Not: "Did I freak you out?" or "Bet I scared you, didn't I!" No one is to blame here. There is no patient zero, no infection. Harvey and I have agreed to take this trip together. We will go on to find submission and surrender on a route that takes us from The Steamworks to family Seders and back again. I'll stop here and leave the sights along the road for you to imagine along with Harvey and Darren and me and so many other exiles who have struggled to find a home in the erotic collective only to become tenants of the psyche's deed of ownership.

15

ASAF

I Am Yourself

EYAL ROZMARIN

EDITOR'S INTRODUCTION

The collective dimension of history and life projects manifests also in Rozmarin's account of a session with Asaf. Highlighting a theme apparent elsewhere in this book, he speaks to the problems of parenting in a world where shared loyalty means shared danger, especially insofar as "to be means to belong." Within this transference–countertransference dynamic, Rozmarin gives an account of how, for better or worse, frank political difference makes its way into the classically neutral space of clinical psychoanalysis. Drawing, like other essays here, on interdisciplinary thought, he presents us with the dilemma of civilized barbarism: To give it up means to suffer disorientation.

A while ago, a few of us, Israelis who live in New York and others on a visit from Israel, gathered for an evening at the New York house of a friend. A conversation developed about whether parents have influence on the choices their children make. We asked ourselves, more specifically, whether parents could, or in fact should, try to persuade their children against army service. The question came up because there was a teenage boy among us, and because we were all in agreement that the Israeli army has been for a long time the tool of questionable politics. It came up, also, because we all knew about the practical and ethical catastrophes and traumas inflicted by and upon young Israelis during their army service. All the same, we had deep doubts that our generation had the ability, or responsibility, to intervene, even as our children face this daunting prospect.

There were two major reasons given as to why parents may eventually stand back. One was in the register of collective identity. As Israelis, some argued, we are responsible for our collective's survival and have to accept such sacrifice. We have to do so in recognition that, despite our misgivings, our children's service is needed to sustain our collective life. The second reason had to do with the realities of parenting. By the time children become teenagers, social belonging and group identity take precedence over family loyalties. Even if parents could resist, most of them would hesitate. We all need to belong. And in Israel, if you are Jewish, belonging still means adopting a certain national ethos, part of it being a soldier—whether we like it or not.

The conversation moved on, but not long after we found ourselves playing a game called Holocaust Alphabet. It goes like this: You go over the alphabet, and for each letter you recall something that has to do with the Holocaust. A goes without saying: Auschwitz, and of course *Arbeit Macht Frei*. B, Bergen Belzen. C, crematorium. D, Dachau. E, Eichman. You get the idea. There is enough to go from A to Z many times.

A stranger will not understand it, but for us this game is great fun. We play it excited and joyful, undoing the weight of our dinner conversation with the lightness of our peculiar version of remembering things past. It brings out the mix of irony and tragedy that is such a familiar aspect of who we are. But, of course, it is more than that. Following a conversation in which we concluded that our children will be sacrificed, it summoned from the depths of our collective psyche the rationale for this sacrifice. Generation after generation, dating back to Abraham, Sarah, and Isaac, our families have been pried open by foreign commands. Having just experienced our helplessness as history asserts itself over our own families, we dream up the moment in which this helplessness emerged most traumatically in our recent past. And between our conversation about the present and our memory tournament, a tragic story asserted itself as the ongoing truth of our lives. We have been, and remain, victims of history, unable to resist the fatal course onto which the next generation will now march. I was reminded of this evening a few months later after a difficult session with a patient.

Asaf is a 40-year-old man whom I have been seeing in my New York office. He grew up in an Israeli kibbutz—that experiment in deconstructing the family that replaced parents with night-nannies and siblings with cohorts. He remembers crying alone at night, quietly, so as to not wake the other children. He also remembers nightly escapes from the children's house to where his parents lived, a distance of a few hundred yards. Scary voyages in the dark, shadows lurking behind trees, wolves howling in the distance—always ending in his being taken back. He was 2 or 3 years old at the time. In the afternoons Asaf often went to visit his grandfather. He was the favorite grandson. Asaf's grandfather came to Palestine as a young man, soon after the war in Europe ended. He spent most of his teenage years in the Warsaw Ghetto and in Auschwitz.

As was expected of him, at 18, Asaf joined an elite unit of the Israeli army. He spent much of his service in south Lebanon and the occupied Palestinian territories. There were frightening moments and cruel reality all around him, but he still does not like to talk about it. There is a strong policy, a "don't ask don't tell me how terrible it is what you go through in the army," between parents and their soldier children. This policy is so powerful that even those who lived through harrowing times together hardly ever talk about it. It is strong enough to force silence many miles and years away, even between patient and therapist.

It is part of the Israeli social contract that trauma is acknowledged collectively but forbidden recognition between individuals. There is a day a year when everyone stops to remember the dead and the wounded and to tell stories of heroism. But personal memories of hardship or protest are considered unpatriotic whining. The same is true for the Israeli arch-trauma, the Holocaust. There is a day a year dedicated to sacred collective commemoration. On the side of the profane, Israeli politicians never hesitate to exploit the Holocaust to support their policies. But those who came to Palestine in the years immediately after this, always personal catastrophe, were consigned to nightmares and silence. Their repression was second only to that applied to the stories of the exiled Palestinians whose land they settled. Asaf's grandfather did not tell him until much later what he had gone through in the Ghetto and in Auschwitz. But what pain was absorbed, what lessons were taken? What connections were drawn in the mind of a child between the silence of his most intimate kin and the loud ethos of the new, über-phallic, Israeli manhood?

The main theme of our work has been to relieve Asaf from the grasp of a cruel dialectic: on one hand a strong wish to be free, to desire without boundaries; on the other a desperate need for ruthless self-mastery. This dilemma, we thought, harkened back to the 2-year-old, crying in vain or gathering himself night after night to search for his parents. This boy was still torn between desperate longing and a dissociative courage that only reaffirmed his loneliness. This boy also carried with him an untold burden, the legacy of his closeness with his grandfather. The secrets that his grandfather spared his children and grandchildren—they lived inside Asaf. They begged him to move on but held him hostage. Recently it felt as if this tug-of-war was driving him insane.

One day in January 2009 Asaf came and said, "I am tired; I can't go on like this. I want to go back to Israel." This was not a new thought. It came up before and we talked about it, but on that day there was a new element in the picture. Israel has just attacked Gaza. He said that he was sorry to see all the destruction, but it was necessary to stop the rockets regularly launched from there. I said I thought the war was wrong. Two criminal governments, indifferent to the lives of helpless people, trapped without recourse. "But they are shooting at us," he said. "But we have been robbing them for decades," I answered, "and then locked them behind wired fences and put them under siege." "We have no choice," he said. "We have other choices," I answered. "They want to destroy us," he said. "But we are much stronger ..." It went on and on. At some point time was up, and we were already standing. Turning to leave the room, Asaf waved his hand and said, "You are crazy."

I was left upset. The war in Gaza had stirred in me a mix of helplessness and outrage, and I just had another opportunity to experience it. But I was also shaken, I literally found myself fighting with a patient. It was not that I regretted it. There was a moment of hesitation, and in that moment I had an instinct that it would be good for us if I jumped in. But now my clinical alarms were ringing. Have I deserted him when he needed me to be reasonable, to hold to what we call thirdness? Did I not, instead, turn into yet another person driven by the circumstances into madness? He said, "You are crazy." Crazy is not what he needs me to be.

Underneath the clinical self-questioning, a far more visceral alarm was ringing. It rang this: Right as you may think you are, you have just taken yourself out of a crucial consensus. On this day, when almost the entire Jewish Israeli population bonds together, you are exposing yourself as a member of a marginal minority—not only marginal but also impotent. You, against the soldiers risking their lives so that your loved ones could live safely, in a protest that has no chance of having an effect. He identifies with them; he longs to be with them. Did he not say this very day that he wanted to go back? You, on the other hand, don't. You never felt a part of their fraternity. Now he knows that you do not belong. Not a good place for the transferential father, to be found out a stranger in the world.

There it was—the specter of a parent's fate in the family that Asaf and I created. In time of trouble, his life in adolescent turmoil, Asaf wanted to go back, to join the other boys in the extended military that Israel was that January. But I became alarmed. What he saw as reassuring, I saw as surrendering to the particular rendering of the collective story that haunted his life. A great fear came up in me that he was pulled against his interest, to seek a dangerous destiny. A destiny that was inscribed in him during his nightly journeys, deepened by his love to his grandfather, and sealed when as a soldier he suffered the evils of war. To be an Isaac without a god or father ever to save him. So I resisted, I tried to protect him by arguing against the war and its false premises. He looked at me as many boys surely look at their parents. "You are crazy," he said, and closed the door.

Could this be what parents face, what they try to avoid—to be seen by their children as pitiful losers in the balance of power among family, child, and society? To be seen by their children as clueless outcasts in a collective that basks safely in its convictions? Could it be that parents let their children go to escape, for their own sake and for the sake of their children, a crisis of identity without resolution?

Walter Benjamin said that, there is no document of civilization which is not at the same time a document of barbarism. Working with Asaf I think we came upon one of the battlegrounds of this civilized barbarism. In this battle, the collective reaches and grasps at the very heart of the subject, making him a hostage of its ideology. Its ground is the tender junction where one's very sense of self draws meaning from collective renderings of life and history. In this junction, Asaf's love for his grandfather is one with the belief instilled in him that a merciless Israel is necessary to save him from a second Holocaust. His ancient longing to be a boy whose parents cared for him masks as nostalgia to a past whose trauma is muted. His fantasy of personal happiness is the subject of national ethos. To be means to belong.

It is the same battleground that opened between the two acts of the evening I described earlier. The memory of the Holocaust came up, casting a spell with the charm of a child's game, to remind us all where we come from. It came to make us forget any objection to the sacrifice now demanded of our families. It came to bind us and at the same time numb us, and we loved it for ridding us of our dilemma. To give it up would surely mean a great deal of loss and disorientation.

But giving up this spell is precisely what is needed. For Asaf to live his life he must somehow untie the knot the makes him long for absent parents and answer to the ghosts that haunt the void he still meets every night. By ghosts I mean not only those of the departed but also those, far more insidious, that carved the texts on their tombstones. These ghosts of history and politics—of history *as* politics, who nationalized their death, made it collective property, and told us how it should become our purpose. These ghosts need to be exposed and exorcized. We need to see how they arise and gravitate between us, how they contrive to make us blind perpetrators of our traumatic past. We need to claim what we wish for and send the draft letters they hand us back. Then, we might be able to ask new questions. Can we be brothers without being brothers in arms? Can we be sons while not abiding by the truths our parents still believe in? What kind of parents can we be? Will I accept a son who wants to go; will he accept a son who clings to him? What might our lives be like if we were not the victims of our history?

16

DeShawn

Beyond the Color Blindness in Gender

AVGI SAKETOPOULOU

EDITOR'S INTRODUCTION

Multiple interpellations operate on any subject any time, a richness that is opportunity and dilemma. Saketopoulou's account of her work with DeShawn in a hospital setting skillfully traces race and gender, sanity and madness, clinical and social hierarchy as they tangle in the mind and body of a psychotic, African American, trans boy. Struggling to maintain her own balance as she takes on a case the hospital staff initially kept from her in the name of encouraging DeShawn's masculinity, Saketopoulou recounts how her work with him changed. She comes to see how her support for his trans identity and longings mixes unpredictably with a potent mix of race, gender, and the complications of racism that she had previously known nothing about.

I have barely stepped onto the inpatient unit to pick up DeShawn for our first session when I see him running towards me. His body slams into mine, and he violently pulls my hair with all the strength his 9-year-old body can muster. "I swear, I'll pull it all out," he screams. I tear up from the pain and crouch down to his height. Now our noses nearly touch and I feel like I can almost taste the smell of his breath; droplets of his sweat land on my skin as he thrashes about. "I know you want to have long hair, that you're angry and scared," I say; my interpretation releases neither my hair from his grip nor DeShawn from his rage. As the staff intervenes to whisk him away, a thick bunch of my hair is clasped in his small black fists.

This incident occurred 3 years into my relationship with DeShawn, which began when he was first admitted to our inpatient unit following multiple prior short-term hospitalizations. At the time of admission he was 7, already diagnosed with schizoaffective disorder: When manic, he was sexually inappropriate and physically injurious to others and himself; when psychotic, he was thought-disordered and would hallucinate.

Spattering his weighty clinical record were also clinicians' derisive references to his cross-gender identifications and "sissy-like" behaviors. DeShawn had wanted to be a girl from as early as his family recalled, and he'd always gestured and walked in ways hailed as effeminate. On the unit, staff was transphobically disturbed by his gender presentation but also genuinely protective of his being bullied or shamed by peers (see Brill & Pepper, 2008; Lev, 2004; Walton, 2005). Adopting a "viral" approach to his gender (Stoller, 1966, 1968, 1975), they informally decided to encourage masculine identifications by keeping him from socializing with female patients. Staff's admonitions that he "act like a man" emerged early on and fed DeShawn's shame, layering onto his preexisting low self-esteem born of illness and hospitalizations; their reluctance to touch him intensified his self-representation as disgusting and abject.

Most of this struggle remaining unmentalized (Fonagy & Target, 1996), DeShawn's hair emerged as the site where his gender transgressions became negotiated with others. He began making wigs: He would staple a piece of paper into a circle and then attach strands of string to its periphery. The wig draped over his head; the strings mimicked hair brushing his shoulders that, girlishly, he would then tuck behind his ears. Staff's upset equaled his elation; either they would take the wig away, or, mysteriously, between bedtime and morning, it would vanish. To restore some semblance of control, DeShawn began compulsively destroying his wigs, biting staff, and becoming self-abusive. His nonnormativity put the unit in disarray, which no amount of psychoeducation* could contain.

---

* I am thinking here of contemporary psychoanalytic theory, which has deconstructed essentialist conceptions of gender challenging the idea that female–male are neatly separated categories (Corbett, 1996, 1997, 2009; Dimen, 1991, 2007; Goldner, 1991, 2006; Harris, 2005, 2008).

It was then that DeShawn came up with an ingenious solution that heralded the emergence of an unanticipated dyadic interrelation between gender and race: He resignified his stringed strands as "dreadlocks." This discursive drag freed the wig from feminine inscriptions, rendering it acceptable, and he was now allowed to wear it. A previously rejected request that he grow his hair was granted on the condition that he braid it. His rage subsided, the unit calmed down, and, while his psychosis did not resolve, he became less thought-disordered and more organized, and his assaultiveness diminished in both frequency and intensity.

Overall, however, and following on the long, sad tradition of conceptualizing trans experience as delusional and pathognomonic of schizophrenia (Caldwell & Keshavan, 1991; Laufer, 1991; Siomopoulos, 1974), clinicians managed their countertransferential anxieties about his gender by attributing it to his psychosis. DeShawn was seen as a boy who wanted to be a girl because he was a *disturbed* boy, despite the fact that his gender remained stable even as psychotropic interventions alleviated some of the psychosis. Psychiatric diagnosis made his subjectivity dismissible, discounting his right to a serious consideration of his gendered experience (McRuer, 2006).

The experiential gap between internal gender fluidity and the rigid regulation of gender prescribed by culture can be profoundly disorienting even for a robustly constituted ego (DiCeglie, 1998a, 1998b, 1998c). For a child's ego, however, it may prove impossible to withstand the pressures of gender-normative expectations. Given that a nascent ego is called upon to tackle multiple developmental challenges, especially when it is, as in DeShawn's case, constitutionally porous to psychopathology, a break with reality may become the only psychic mechanism through which the misalignment between psyche and culture can be tolerated. In other words, deeming DeShawn's gender a manifestation of his illness did more than just marginalize him: *It fenced him into his psychosis.* Consequently, when, long before I became his therapist, he'd seek me out, I would gladly engage his interest in dolls and makeup, even though staff feared "it would encourage his belief and make him more hypersexual."

Our bond became strong and intimate. When bullied, he'd run to me, press his head against my belly, and cry inconsolably. My hair, representing his fantasy of uncomplicated femininity, was central. He'd gently tug on it as he sobbed, and sometimes, before I could stop him, stuff it into his mouth like a famished infant gobbling the nipple. This regressively desirous relationship to my hair contrasted with his barbaric yanking of it before our first play therapy session, an act that had confused and wounded me. Not surprisingly, given his passion, once we started play therapy, I found DeShawn's play to be anything but stilted, a finding that contrasts with reports of gender-variant boys' play as joyless and compulsive (Coates & Moore, 1998). Rummaging through bags of toys, he discarded Black dolls before choosing a White one with long, luscious, silky hair. Placing her on top of a fan, he giggled joyfully as her tresses playfully tangled in the wind.

Such moments were not only gendered but also saturated in *racial* meanings. I wondered whether gender was being appropriated by racialized self-hatred. Was he any different from those Black schoolchildren who, Kenneth Clark taught us, preferred White to Black dolls (Klueger, 2004)? Or had DeShawn folded race *into* gender? As a Black boy growing up in a culture where ideals of femininity are hued in White, was femininity for him *at odds with* his Blackness?

These thoughts circulated in my mind for several months into our work before DeShawn took from my toy shelf a big, stuffed teddy bear wearing a pink wig, which he had previously ignored. He tried it on, looking at himself in the mirror; "I'm beautiful," he said proudly. In that moment he no longer was the insecurely effeminate child I'd known; his girliness became something to delight over. I imagined him as a vibrant, radiant, girly performer singing, "I will survive," the audience cheering him on: drag queen extraordinaire! My reverie saw his creativity and resilience: its significance did not hinge on how his atypical gender would carry him into adulthood but in that the hope for his happiness, for a life outside institutional walls had been possible to imagine. "Yes, you are *so* beautiful," I said, moved by his joy.

"I'm sorry I pulled your hair that day," he said. "That was the day that Paul [a staff member who had made it his personal project to make a man out of DeShawn] said I gotta keep it real and get a haircut." "You didn't want to disappoint him," I said, recalling how hard he'd worked to be allowed to grow it out. "No!" DeShawn corrected me, "*I* [he emphasized the *I*], *I* gotta keep it real."

DeShawn's crisp response spoke something new; condensed in it was not just a gender imperative, but a *gender imperative spoken in Ebonics*. What was really at stake here was not masculinity but racial identification. The kind of "man" that Paul implored my patient to be wasn't merely rigidly gendered—it was raced. My patient had on some level been keenly aware of, perhaps even shared, the racial anxieties underlying the staff's fears. My previous attention to transphobia had blinded me to the racial demands on DeShawn's gender. Caught up in a White discourse that treats masculinity as a prized possession, I missed that *for Black boys racial identification trumps gender anytime* (Perry, 2002). Where White teenage boys taunt one another for being "a faggot," Black adolescents' offense is "acting White" (Pascoe, 2007).

The non-White staff had responded to my nonpathologizing of DeShawn's atypical gender as a form of racist emasculation. This response is embedded in the historical discourse of attacks on Black masculinity, from actual castrations to the symbolic emasculation of Black men denied paternity rights and male entitlements by their White slave owners (hooks, 2004; Neal, 2006), which sedimented nonnormativity in a racial matrix. "Homosexuality," says Julien in his famous *Looking for Langston*, "is a sin against the race," an idea birthing the notion that those who are gay cannot possibly be authentically black (West, 1993). The economics of reproduction in the colonial period favored "breeder women" who were afforded the protections of not being sold (Collins, 2005), thus consolidating the survival value of heterosexuality (Cole & Guy-Sheftal, 2003). When the 1863 American Freedman's Inquiry Commission situated newly emancipated slaves in the state, it made American citizenship contingent on (heterosexual) marriage by deeming extramarital unions as emblematic of the "uncivilized, degraded … ways of the slaves" (Ferguson, 2004, p. 86). The idea that homosexuality compromises masculinity cuts across racial lines, but for Black Americans it carries the additional burden of imperiling racial membership.

There was nothing spectacular in how these thoughts influenced my work as they slowly worked their way into my time with DeShawn. Having a way to linguistically represent the continuities between race and gender and therefore to be able to think them, I found myself entertaining questions that pertained less to his gendered and racial experience as based on static, distinct systems and more to how they are and might be braided together. Of this, though, I said very little if anything at all. Mostly, I was able to now nod encouragingly as my patient anxiously turned to me when his play would venture into racio-gendered territory. Where I'd have previously commented on it as distinctively raced or gendered, I now stopped disrupting him from playing, playing out, and dwelling on their tangled meanings.

17

LYNN, BEN, LUCY

Forbidden To Be

OLGA PUGACHEVSKY

EDITOR'S INTRODUCTION

"Great American dreams are imported American dreams," says Pugachevsky in this essay on her work with immigrant patients. An immigrant herself, she considers the impact of the "subcollective" on her and her patients, and the "false self" with which her patients live. Variously successful with them, she reflects on the goals of psychoanalysis in a context in which, for patients and their parents, doing becomes more important than being and on how enhancing and healing it would be were her patients to recognize and value unproductive desire.

It is my opinion that it is certainly "better to be alive, real and mad than to live from the False Self" (Hopkins, 2000). Here the "false self" signifies a cluster of those self-states that are not springing from or even partaking of one's desire but whose main characteristic is a lack, a cold lacunae at their very core. In spite of possibly highly productive functioning and busy social schedule the feeling the person conveys is that of emptiness, of his or her desire asleep, or unborn, or dead. There are many routes to this point of nonbeing, but those three people that I am going to introduce went, or better to say were taken, down the same road. One was far gone, the second somewhere in the middle, and the third just starting. The first one got herself back, the second is getting himself back, and the third ... I lost her.

Enter Lynn, a highly paid professional, with her springy step, bright smile, silvery bubbling chat, a pen and a notebook in her hand, a perfect picture of sprightly efficiency. Well, Lynn got all my red flags up right away because … she bored me. And thus, I knew that something was seriously off. It took me six sessions to gently introduce the subject. I said something like, "You know it's really strange; you told me already a lot about yourself, but somehow I don't feel who you are." She shrugged: "One is what one does, right?" "Just that?" I asked. "What else?" she said.

The crux of the matter—"What else?" It was a real "what," with no space for a "who," and even for that meager "what" there was no "else." No space beyond sheer doing, *being* rejected as frivolous, illegitimate, unthinkable, evoking unbearable anxiety. There was only her constant striving to achieve, and with it her constant dutiful worrying about achieving. She was a success story, a pride and joy of her family, the one who made the family itself an object of jealousy in its community.

Ben, a college student, was brought in by his mother. The mother said, "Do you think you could fix him, or he is always going to stay like this?"

"Like what?"

"Just look at him!"

Ben was slumping in a chair, his skinny arms and legs limp, mutely looking at the opposite wall. It was not an understandable angry silence of a teenager dragged by his parent to a doctor he did not care about but something that felt like a bottomless inertia, some deep paralyses of will.

"We, his father and I, are killing ourselves to pay for his college, and he is failing everything. Everybody is laughing at us. But he just doesn't care about us. I can't understand how one could be so heartless! And he used to be such a good student in junior high."

So in this tangled emotional universe Ben's poor grades meant not that he possibly had ceased to care about his own life but that somehow he stopped caring about his parents, who in turn did not care so much about Ben himself as about his grades. And also somehow "everybody" was in the picture as well as obviously his parents' shame was. And another important piece—Ben used to be what his family wanted.

I met Lucy when she was a pale 7-year-old girl who sat quite still during my conversation with her mother, not looking at us, not asking for anything, just sitting in a chair with her little hands folded in her lap. The mother said that she went against the whole family bringing her daughter to consult me because there was no real trouble. Lucy got perfect grades in everything and excelled in her after-school activities. "But," her mother said, "she often complains that she is bored and gets very whiny that way."

Actually it quickly turned out that Lucy was in a really serious trouble, because at 7 years of age she could not play.

These three patients of mine had a theme in common, for they were struggling with the most fundamental issue of all—the legitimacy of permitting themselves just to be.

And they shared one other thing—they were the second generation of immigrants from Eastern Europe and growing up in the families determined to make them achieve the Great American Dream. The irony is that most American Dreams are imported American Dreams, so to speak.

What kind of a family would uproot itself from all its traditions, connections, from all the safety nets spun over generations and go to a faraway unknown place? It is a family of people who can in some way imagine such a place, can fantasize a projection of their future, worth the tremendous effort and pain of immigration.

Ah, family. If one looks closely one can conceive of a family as a tiny collective within a larger one, that larger collective being not the Great collective of the society in general but a subcollective defined by class, race, history, geography, and myriad other characteristics. As the Great collective is defined by its discourse, so the subcollective is defined by its specific discourse. Necessarily the two discourses are intricately intertwined, but they are not the same.

When a family dreams it dreams in terms of the discourse of its subcollective.

The immigration fantasy is an old dream, and the script usually spans two generations. It necessitates the parents' sacrifice, since they have to give up everything that is familiar and stable, likely lose their social status, and consent to become the springboard for their children. In turn the children accept the obligation to achieve and live the parents' dream, not their own, so the parents can be fulfilled vicariously through their offspring's success.

Trying to build an old fantasy in the new world is like trying to translate a poem or a joke word for word. It just does not work. The dream has to be rewritten from scratch to be rooted in the discourse of the new society. But the act of rewriting might question the parents' sacrifice, so it becomes off limits.

Thus first a dream, then a hope, then a project, terms getting more rigid as losses and hardships accumulate, evolves, until finally it becomes a sacred goal never to be questioned or reexamined. Reality is not allowed, the family discourse is artificially cut off from the discourse of the new society. If you can pass for a WASP (White Anglo-Saxon Protestant) and have perfect scores, then you will achieve what is required; if you are not there yet, it just means that you are not trying hard enough. The cost of failure is so high and the fear of it so great that the new generation is brought up solely "to do," not "to be." Thus, to get to the top, Cinderella—and not her evil sister—has to cut off half of her foot to fit into the glass slipper. Sorry, my mistake, half of her heart.

To put it a little differently, a collective discourse that allows no space for recognition of "unproductive" personal strivings and desires shadowed my patients' individual development resulting in their forgetting, repressing, and finally dissociating the very core of their personhood. Ogden (1995) said:

> The goal of analysis … is larger than that of the resolution of unconscious intrapsychic conflict, the diminution of symptomatology, the enhancement of reflective subjectivity and self-understanding, and the increase of the sense of personal agency. Although one's sense of being alive is intimately intertwined with each of the above mentioned capacities, I believe that the experience of aliveness is a quality superordinate to these capacities and must be considered as an aspect of the analytic experience in its own terms. (p. 696)

In all three cases I found myself turned into a sort of supersensitive playful mother searching for signs of life in a seemingly comatose child: an interested glance here, a smile there, a sign, a gesture, a dream. Every tiny spark of life to be noticed, nurtured, built up. And, ah, the first playful interaction, the first joke perhaps—signs of life, of the budding ability to be that then ushers in creativity, spontaneous gesture, authentic personal agency, and capacity for symbolization.

Lynn's awakening started with a dream. She dreamed that she gave birth to a baby girl whom she did not know how to feed. Her mother entered the room and suggested to breastfeed the baby, but my patient saw that her mother's nipples were sharp bony things and did not give the baby to her. This theme continued, and so Lynn's dreams about her having a baby girl and being able to feed her more and more successfully became sort of marks of our progress. Gradually, very painfully, with many starts and stops, she learned to pay attention to herself, to "hear" herself, to care about herself. She learned to allow herself to be funny, playful, to do things just because she wanted to, and to protect all that from her family, real and imaginary. She finally allowed herself to fall happily in love for the first time.

As it turned out, Ben used to be a very "good boy," effortlessly best in his class, until he got to a high school for gifted students, where he could not be the best anymore. Pushed and reprimanded by his parents, tormented by his own shame and guilt, and still unable to repeat his former achievements, he essentially gave up. At the beginning our work was slow, laborious, full of interminable silences. We found out that Ben could not experience anything directly but only deduce from what he was doing. "Well, if I did that thing it means that I felt like it, right? Otherwise why would I do it?" Sometimes he asked me, "So what am I feeling?" Then there came a day when he said, "It's like, it's like ... nobody ever saw me ... for real, I mean." He put it very well: No one in his family ever wanted to notice Ben the person but saw only Ben the project. He is doing much better now; we are still walking.

And Lucy was the one I lost. I saw her only a few times. She started to trust me a little and to veer from the repetitive enactment of her own boring day when playing with my dollhouse. She accepted a magic possibility of two cows visiting her school during the lunch break, the white one giving the regular milk and the brown one the chocolate, and even added her own little embellishment to the tale. She even smiled once. But then her mother called me to let me know that Lucy began to want her attention too much, that she did not see how playing with dolls could be useful, and that she wanted to get her daughter advanced math tutoring, which would leave no time or money to continue therapy. Yes, she said, she knew that her daughter was sort of depressed, but Lucy was getting perfect grades, she behaved, and what more could anyone want, and if she grows up not so happy, well, it's not a big deal. We didn't get a good-bye session. Lucy, where are you?

18

MARTHA

Resignification Road

GLENYS LOBBAN

EDITOR'S INTRODUCTION

Lobban's discovery of her own mixed racial heritage finds its clinical expression in her story of her treatment of Martha. It becomes key to a twist made central by many contemporary clinical accounts: Her anxiety about her own history creates a countertransference enactment whose recognition allows her patient to blossom. As she details this process for us, she shows us, once again, how important social forces are in the clinical setting and how valuable to psychoanalysis are concepts from social and cultural thought, not only, once again, interpellation, but also hybridity, multiculturalism, and multiracialism.

The family plonks gaudy beach towels down on the hot sand. The Indian Ocean stretches before them; undulating navy blue crests, fringed by angry whirlpools of white foam that pound the golden glistening sand. "Race you to the water," yells the dark-haired girl. "But what about the sharks, Mom?" asks the blond daughter. "Are there shark nets here?"

The Mom replies, "Go ahead and swim, honey; the water looks great. Forget about the sharks. You won't be attacked unless it is your day to be attacked. And you know, if it is your day, nothing you do can change that. People think they can escape fate by just staying put on their beach mat, but if it is their day, something will lure them into the water, like seeing a kid knocked down by a wave and rushing in to help." The girls are totally reassured, and they race into the warm water, squealing with excitement.

That was Margaret, my mother, speaking. She taught me life lessons that were completely different from those endorsed by the other "White" South African mothers in our lush neighborhood. Those mothers favored rationality above all else, whereas my mother believed in astrology and eagerly consulted her horoscope every day. Ours was also the only White household where the dead grandmother was a regular visitor. Whenever my mother was seriously upset by events in her life and in need of help, she would sense her dead mother's presence in the room. (I was always relieved that Nellie, my grandmother, didn't actually physically materialize in our living room at one of my mother's weekly séances. I am sure my pragmatic Scots father felt similar relief.)

My mother was deeply attached to Nellie and invoked her constantly. Nellie's personality and values infused my childhood, though she died when I was only 8 months old. We all lived in Nellie's orbit and knew her story. My grandmother was my childhood heroine. Nellie was a survivor. She was tragically widowed at the age of 30 and raised her two tiny children alone. She struggled with poverty all her adult life, yet she remained passionate, optimistic, and generous. Her spirituality kept her buoyant. She was a devout Episcopalian who sang in the church choir every Sunday morning. Nellie was also a medium, with the gift of second sight, so on Sunday nights she and her children regularly attended séances.

Four years ago my mother, who was dying of cancer in South Africa, confessed to us that her mother Nellie was biracial. My grandmother was "Eurasian," a mix of a father who was European and a mother with South Asian slave roots. (See "White or Not," this volume, where I describe her background in more detail.) Nellie's Eurasian mother passed as White from 1894, when she married her English husband in Cape Town and they moved to Johannesburg. My mother figured out the secret when she was about 10 years old; she pieced it together from Nellie's hints. My mother never discussed the secret directly with Nellie or anyone else. When she was a child my mother had often heard her mother say, "There is only one thing about myself that I regret and really wish I could change." Once she knew the secret, she interpreted this lament to mean that her mother Nellie wished she could change her biracial origins and be all White.

Discovering our family secret had a profound impact on me, even though it did not change my actual life circumstances in any way. I was hailed by my mother as "not pure White"; I was interpellated as a person of color. I learned from my response to this news that apparently I believed that White always trumps in the bridge game of life; I had bought into the ideal of "Whiteness" (Altman, 2000, 2004, 2006; Harris, 2007a, 2007b; Straker, 2004, 2006, 2007; Suchet, 2004, 2007; see also my chapter "White or Not" in this volume.)

Judith Butler (1997) uses the term *resignification* to describe the process whereby a person who is interpellated can break beyond the interpellation. The person reinterprets the social category to which she is assigned and thus redefines it. I am now traveling down "Resignification Road." I am slowly interrogating the labels Eurasian and "not White," stripping off their racist patina to paint them in rainbow hues. My journey has rendered race, ethnicity, and difference more salient for me.

As I processed my feelings about our family secret, I kept thinking about the toll that keeping the secret for all those years took on my mother. My mother was strikingly beautiful, witty, smart, and charismatic, but a sinkhole of insecurity lurked just beneath the surface. As a child I tried to understand her porous self-esteem. I explained it in terms of her class origins, the fact that she was raised in poverty by a single mother. Now I know another source of her fragility and brittleness. My mother was raised as White in Apartheid South Africa, where racial and ethnic differences were constantly identified and Whiteness was the yardstick of status and privilege. She herself internalized racism, and then she had to somehow come to terms with the fact that her own, beloved mother was not White but biracial as that this meant that my mother was also not White.

I was working with a biracial woman patient, whom I will call Martha, while I was processing my mother's revelation. (This therapeutic encounter took place in New York where I practice as an analyst. I immigrated to New York when I was 22 years old to escape Apartheid.) Suddenly, a part of our canvas that had previously been in the shadow was illuminated for me. Before I tell you about our silent enactment, I will give you a brief outline of the earlier work with Martha.

Martha is a 30-year-old, college educated, biracial woman, who was raised in Los Angeles in a liberal family. Her White, American father is a public interest lawyer. Her Latina mother was born in the Dominican Republic and teaches children with special needs. When she began treatment, Martha felt guilty because she was closer to her father than her mother. Midway through the treatment, Martha realized that she hungered for a connection with her mother and her Latina roots. She took matters into her own hands and went on a journey of resignification. She broke into her mother's orbit, traveled to the Dominican Republic, lived with her mother's family for 6 months and learned Spanish.

A few months after her trip, Martha began dating a woman, a first for her. Her usually liberal parents, and especially her mother, were slow to warm up to the idea of her homosexual desire. She was describing her frustration about this when a light bulb went on for me. I realized that I had never asked Martha whether her new girlfriend was White or Black or Latina. Actually, Martha had never mentioned the ethnic origins of anyone she talked about in our sessions, whether they were a friend, a lover, or a colleague, and I had remained oblivious. (Most patients do identify ethnicity, particularly if the person they are describing is different from them. They will say, "I have a new lover, but she is not Asian like me; she is White," or "She is Black.") When I finally registered my blind spot and our racial enactment (Leary, 2000), I asked myself why Martha did not tell about ethnicity and race, and I did not ask.

After I figured out that Martha and I had been weaving a tapestry sans color, some interesting developments occurred in the treatment. I did not talk about the enactment with Martha directly. Instead, when she next mentioned her girlfriend, I said, "What is her cultural background? You have never mentioned anything about it." "She's White, Jewish actually, from Atlanta, Georgia," Martha told me. She then launched into a flood of fascinating information about her Latina mother, things she had never verbalized before. Up till then she had described her mother's difference as if it were a linguistic difference. She would say, "My mother is Spanish, you know, more reserved, uncomfortable at the High School Parents' Association meetings." Now Martha moved to a different register and acknowledged her mother as a person of color.

Martha said, "And you may be right; my girlfriend's background, the fact that she is White, that is part of my mother's problem with her." (I did not interrupt her to point out that I had offered no such hypothesis; I'd merely asked her what her girlfriend's cultural background was.) "You know, Mike was the only boyfriend of mine that she liked, and that is because he is Latino." I asked, "Why would your mother want you to have a Latino boyfriend?"

Martha said, "I think she felt threatened by my seeing a White guy, though that is ridiculous when she is married to a White guy. I know she feels jealous and left out that I am so close to my father. But you know he lets me get close, and she is so hard to get near. She makes herself into an outsider in our family. She is the one who refuses to answer questions about her life in the Dominican Republic or talk Spanish to me. It is her who says we need to be American and speak English. I can't believe how cold she is being about my girlfriend; it hurts me so, and it also makes me so mad. She knows it upsets me, or maybe she doesn't even value herself enough to know how much I long to be close to her."

At this point in the session, Martha dissolved into desperate tears. She had never been so impassioned before. My small question about culture and race spoke volumes and enabled her to repaint her relationship with her mother in Technicolor. Martha told me, "I spent my childhood being in the middle, constantly veering between thinking about one parent then the other, trying to make sure that each of my parents got exactly equal attention from me and that no one hurt my mother's feelings or undervalued her because she was Latina."

Martha and I continued to address her longing to be in an intense, loving relationship with both of her parents. We embarked on a journey into the Oedipal hinterland. I am using the term *oedipal* here to refer to a complete Oedipus complex (the child's desire to simultaneously have a close attachment and an intimate, sexual relationship with her mother and her father, to become like each of them, and to wage a competition with her mother to possess her father, and similar competition with her father, for her mother). I believe that this constellation of wishes related to the parents is always shaped and inflected by culture, and its myriad complex threads manifest as many different self-states. In Martha's case, her journey was shadowed by race, by her experience of her Latina mother as vulnerable and fragile, less robust than her White father.

Martha's smart and successful Latina mother accepted Whiteness as her gold standard, and this leached away her self-esteem and self-confidence. Martha responded to her mother's racialized subjectivity by trying to protect her. She was afraid to compete with her mother lest she injure her further. Martha felt guilty because she had light skin and hair and could pass for White. She solved the problem of her mother's fragility by always staying in her mother's terrain, by her side. She never abandoned her and moved into her father's White sphere. For example, Martha wanted to be a teacher like her mother, she planned to teach high school after she completed her graduate program in international relations, and she never contemplated moving into law, her father's sphere.

Martha's strategy for managing her interracial family was to act as if she was color-blind, to erase race. Why did I go along with Martha? Why did I fail to notice that she left out ethnic origins when she described her cast of characters? My first answer to this question was that there were striking parallels between Martha's stance toward her mother and my attitudes to my mother and this caused me to identify with her and accept her version of reality. Both of us felt guilty about having higher social status than our mothers, and we felt very protective toward them. We evolved different solutions to our guilt, different methods to avoid competition. Martha stayed in her mother's territory and modeled herself after her mother, whereas I vowed to never encroach on any area that my mother prized and allowed myself to excel only in spheres that did not interest my mother or my father, like psychology and left-wing politics.

When I was in the midst of writing this chapter, I realized that this "fragile mothers" explanation was only part of the story of my collusion with Martha. There was another similarity between us: Martha was color-blind at home, and so was I. I elected to be blind to the many clues about our family secret that were hidden in plain sight during my childhood. Nellie, my flamboyant exotic grandmother, with her séances and her astrology, possessed traits that were totally atypical for an English-speaking White South African. In the dominant discourse of Apartheid South Africa, Whites were defined as "Western" and "rational." A belief in spirits, witch doctors, and ancestor worship was the preserve of "Black" people who were supposedly "primitive." I remember noting how different my mother's beliefs were from the beliefs of the mothers of my friends. I wondered why my mother and my grandmother were so eccentric. I just never jumped to the obvious answer: Nellie believed in spirits and fate because these beliefs were passed down from her ancestors of color. In my student activist days in South Africa, we always joked about how many White South Africans were actually of mixed race, but I did not seriously apply this idea to my family. I never for a moment entertained the thought that my "exotic" grandmother might really be exotic; I colluded with Martha's color blindness in the therapeutic relationship because it matched my own.

The interracial family is a locus where all the culture's contradictory messages about race and Whiteness meet head on. These can refract and complicate a biracial child's relationships with both of her parents and her attempts to define her racial subjectivity in a positive way (see Bushra, 2009). Is it possible to redefine the term *biracial* so that it was not predicated on the gold standard of Whiteness? Barack Obama, our first biracial president, gave a wonderful example of such resignification at his first press conference as president-elect (on November 7, 2008). A Chicago reporter asked Obama what type of dog the first family planned to get. Obama replied that he would like to get a dog who was "a mutt like me." The White female reporter who had asked the question visibly grimaced. She was extremely startled because the future president of the United States was referring to himself as a "mutt." Obama embraced the term "mutt" and thus remade it. He connected the idea of being racially "mixed" with the presidency, something everyone admires and aspires to. So perhaps our years with President Obama in office will lead to a new ideal in America: We will all glory in our rainbow, multihued "muttness," and Whiteness will pale by comparison.

LETTERS TO THE AUTHORS

Discussion of "Subjective Experience, Collective Narratives"

ANDREW SAMUELS

"Don't they see anyone normal?" I muttered to myself before wondering what on earth I meant by it. It was not a lack of appreciation for the work and the writing—far from it. But there is extraordinary clinical material presented here, and equally extraordinary analytical dyads have been introduced to us. All the pieces in this section of the book are nothing if not marvelously and unremittingly dramatic and unusual. The work is exciting and gripping and never uninformative. Strange coincidences, overlaps of personal history between analyst and client, secrets of all kinds abound. At times, in my responses, I made deliberate use of this, asking if such work with clients seemingly from the cultural margins was not particularly valuable for general practice in analysis and psychotherapy. But I wanted to flag up here how working with persons in cultural extremes has led to an extreme genre of clinical writing, a subcollective parallel process. Perhaps the quotidian version will come in time.

Before addressing some remarks to the writers one by one, I want to make a few overall observations. I was struck by how undifferent the work was from mainstream relational psychoanalysis (as expressed in the literature) when the political, social, and cultural circumstances of these clients might have been expected to generate more idiosyncratic ways of working to respond to the particular psycho-political detail being presented. But this was not the case, and I wonder about the limiting effect of not actively looking for a plethora of analytical theories and techniques. The emotional reactions of the analysts did seem to me to chime with the clients' exigencies—but not really the ways the analysts worked with and thought about the unconscious.

How strange it would be if, in the middle of all the radical thinking and the reconstruction of psychoanalysis for today's broken political world, there is a secret and persisting one-size-fits-all conservatism in the very enterprise itself.

I felt that these clinical vignettes highlighted that certain themes such as "political selfhood" or "political development" are still under-theorized in psychoanalysis generally. In some of the cases, I found myself wanting to know even more about where they (the analyst and the client) got their politics from, of the relative importance of the politics of father and mother, of the ways social class has operated at an unconscious level, of how we understand the ways in which ethnic, national, and religious factors transmogrify into political attitudes and behaviors, and—in an imaginative return to the bedrock of psychoanalytic exploration—how issues of sex, sexuality, and gender play into the formation of the political subject. Yes, the stories were gripping and amazing. But I believe we need to be careful lest the striking facts of these larger-than-life narratives make us forget that what looks like "facts" are, in common with much political autobiography, more in the nature of personal myth. At times, for me, there were just too many facts in play for me to manage in my mind. The historian E. H. Carr (1964) wrote that "the facts speak only when the historian calls upon them" (p. 7).

A further overall impression concerns what might be called the micro-politics of the session. I missed much that I would expect to find in British books and papers on similar themes about the analyst's power over the client (e.g., Chaplin, 2005). There was much more about the client's influence and even power on the analyst. I believe psychoanalysis still lacks a coherent synchronous political analysis of the power and the vulnerability of both the analyst and the client and how these evolve over the course of an analysis. In general, I think that many analysts have a problem in realizing that they are both powerful and vulnerable—it is not a case of either powerful or vulnerable. In other words, much thinking about who has the power and who has the vulnerability in the politics of the analytical relationship has been rather schizoid.

A concluding reflection: Analyst and patient are nearly always citizens in the same polity. But they will occupy different citizen positions due to economic, cultural, and other differences. Nevertheless, despite such differences, they are linked by social bonds (with the psychological potential for mutual recognition as well as oppression along the lines Jessica Benjamin [1988] mapped out). Would any of us, thinking as psychoanalysts, want to regard the common state of citizenship as it applies to analysts and patients within exclusively social terms? Could it be the case that what makes unconscious to unconscious communication, transference–countertransference dynamics, and therapeutic dialogue *possible* is this shared experience of citizenship? Could it be the political relationship of analyst and patient that leads to their psychological relationship? If this is the case, then what has been located behind the corral fence of the taboo on politics within psychoanalysis has been secretly facilitating our work all along.

To Orna

It's an awesome story, the potlatch gift from your friendly neighborhood sperm donor who gets off on his woman's idea and makes an unwelcome pass. But then the whole drama was suffused with superiority and aggression, wasn't it, most of it denied or attributed to the booze? It's a perfectly horrible story, showing, in a micro-social context, just how the powerful maintain themselves generally. As in the potlatch ritual, a hierarchy is established and maintained. And this is the shadow of philanthropy anyway, and maybe of liberalism generally. Shakespeare got it in *Timon of Athens*: That apparently most generous and giving man demonstrates how, when pressed, he was murderous, misanthropic, and effectively resentful all along.

What changes if we were to take the story on another level, whether developmentally or symbolically, rather than as a narrative that was related in the session? What changes then in our understanding? I wonder about the level of fate of Grace's sexual self-confidence. If there is such a thing as God-given sexual power, was her share a small one? Isn't a baby entitled to a feeling of being irresistible in her sexual self—Hera, Athena, and Aphrodite all in one (the three Goddesses who present to Paris for his choice apple)? The experience of feeling such irresistibility is the archetypal basis of sexual self-esteem.

Perhaps Grace's mother's "reassurance" didn't work because it inevitably missed that level of sexual affirmation. To be honest, I had expected to hear of an actively censorious and repressive mother, and maybe that was what Grace experienced deep down—it is hard to be sure. I am not saying that Grace is in the grip of any specific psychopathology that I can think of. But there may have been a developmental lack in the area of necessary erotic playback from mother to daughter that could have contributed to the depersonalization the two of you were working on. Where is the affirmation of Grace's sexual self to come from? If Grace finds this in the relationship with Lila, it doesn't mean this is the reason for that relationship. But in terms of the maternal mind that you mention, it's the sexual quadrant that's needed, isn't it?

The question that struck me after this thought was how the erotic playback theme was or was not being played out in the transference–countertransference. Here, I was struck by your introduction of some pointed comments concerning interpellation and your experiences of living in Israel, leading to your leaving the country. How, I wondered, does this choice of an example fit with the rest of the clinical material? I'll try to keep this simple, just as the ideas came up in me. It's too pat, I know, so consider this just a reconnaissance: Israel as the mother who cannot admire something in her citizen-daughter, the mother who insists that her own (political-sexual) lacks and limitations be the inheritance of the child. For the distinguishing feature of ideology is its march to conformism. But here, rather than conform, the daughter walks away. As she does so, and settled in the United States, what are her main affects? They'd include anger, perhaps, of which more later, in terms of the client.

Concerning conformism, we know how shattering nonconformist same-sex parents are to the cultural collective, even now, even in Manhattan or Hampstead. There is an onslaught on the prevailing order contained in the phenomenon, which it is fruitless to dispute. I'm not saying that same-sex parents are aiming to carry out an onslaught; they just are doing so—revolution without intent. But just to speak of "onslaught" is to raise sexuality's twin—aggression—and I want now to talk a little about how the angry affects play into dissociation and depersonalization.

We might ask what is the *telos* (goal, aim, purpose) of such symptoms rather than where they come from (see Samuels, 1985, pp. 11, 91). What are they for? What do they help the subject manage? I think that in this instance Grace's relentless pursuit of a state in which "it all went quiet" has as much to do with the management of aggression as with sexuality. Of course, you were limited by space in what you discussed in your piece, Orna, but I am going to fantasize that there were issues for Grace in reconciling the woman she felt she should be (in terms of her mother's values) with aggressive thoughts, feelings, fantasies, and impulses.

Israel nudges in again, but not in terms of Israeli aggression—more in terms of the unsettling cultural paradox of physically aggressive Jews as opposed to timid scholars. The parallel is with the way images of aggressive women challenge the social order. Whether it's about sex or aggression, I think you're saying that analyst and client both have the "conditions of possibility" making it possible to leave the mother(land)s' world.

To Steve

I'm going to steal the profound issues you raise in the paper for all therapy, not just as relevant to a situation where there's a gay analyst and a gay client and an overlapping of sexperiences. For the things you have had to work out with Harvey and Darren confirm that the most important developments taking place in psychotherapy generally are at what are laughably called "the margins." All the pressures you write about—self-disclosure, incest-fueled general sexual states in the countertransference, struggles to dis-identify from the life narrative of the Other whose life is, to be blunt, not the same as the analyst's life—these are (or should be) the struggle of every contemporary psychotherapist (Samuels, 1999, unpublished).

There's a "serious injustice" in the theories and values of much psychoanalysis, not just in human life (which was what your quotation from Freud was referring to). It is interesting to note how often discussions about promiscuity even in quite liberal professional circles of psychotherapists collapse into discussions about promiscuous cruising (cottaging in British usage) on the part of gay men. I have been arguing for many years that therapists have been unconsciously influenced by the media and collective cultural discourses as much as by psychoanalytic theories (past and present) concerning the general psychopathology of homosexuality. They have got caught up in a moral panic concerning cottaging and haven't noticed that they've allowed heterosexual promiscuity to fall out of the conversation. Hence, it is well-nigh impossible to manage a reasoned conversation about either promiscuity or cottaging. Is this the wider collective anxiety that played into your insistent and unmanageable concern about Darren's barebacking? An interpellative experience for you as a "responsible" analyst?

I'd like to propose a few rather different ideas to the ones you develop in your piece based on the general idea that promiscuity is not only a literal matter. It is also implicated in a whole array of imaginative and metaphorical discourses. In addition to the political symbolism of challenging normative monogamy, we can think of promiscuity as symbolizing boundary-breaking creativity in both an artistic and a general sense. Barebacking may perhaps be a most extreme example of this general point.

From a nonliteral point of view, promiscuity calls up symbolic or metaphorical dimensions of issues of freedom, differentiation from parental and family background, and a new relation to the primal scene. Even with bodies in mind, there is still a metaphorical aspect to promiscuous sex. Promiscuous traces and shadows may be present in constant sexual relationships via the operation of fantasy, and there may be a constant element in apparently promiscuous behavior, if the image of the sexual Other remains psychically constant. This takes us back to the Freud–Jung schism over sexuality. Freud spoke for the literal, the instinctual, the causative; Jung for the metaphorical and the teleological, asking "what is sex really for?" Sexual imagery is not only a desire for physical enactment. It is also a symbolic expression of an emotional longing for some kind of personal regeneration through contact with the body of an Other. As Philip Roth (2001, p. 15) said, "The great biological joke on people is that you are intimate before you know anything about the other person."

It is significant that sex outside of relationship is largely untheorized by analysts and therapists—or, if there is a theoretical position taken, it is invariably in terms of psychopathology, of an alleged fear of intimacy, problems in attachment ("ambivalent attachment") and relationship, perversion, and so on. There is an absence of consideration of what Muriel Dimen (1995) referred to as sex-as-force not sex-as-relation (p. 158). We have learned that, for every majority discourse, there is likely to be a subjugated minority discourse. In psychotherapy—as in society—the majority discourse is relational. Hence, the subjugated minority discourse will be the opposite of relational: promiscuous (see Samuels, 2010).

I will end with something you may find mad. I felt an absence in your paper of what was going on at depth when the clients undertook self-destructive behaviors that you responded so strongly to. What was going on? I don't think psychodynamics gets the whole picture. No, there is a spiritual piece to consider. (I say that there are three sides to the coin: psyche, the social/cultural, and the spiritual.)

This kind of sexual behavior may be understood in terms of mystical experience. There's something numinous about risk-taking promiscuous experience, as we all know. Overwhelming physical attraction produces feelings of awe and wonderment and trembling. There is a sort of God aroused, a primitive, chthonic, early, elemental God. There is an unfettered experience of the divine.

The idea of a mysticism between people is one by which contemporary theology is captivated. "There is no point at all in blinking at the fact that the raptures of the theistic mystic are closely akin to the transports of sexual union," wrote Richard Zaehner in *Mysticism: Sacred and Profane* (1957, p. 111). More recently, in a series of works Robert Goss (e.g., Goss, 2004, p. 59) has been suggesting that behind nonmonogamous relating we find the presence of a "promiscuous God," one who loves indiscriminately (if hardly casually). Although Goss is primarily concerned with the reclamation of the bible for lesbian, gay, bisexual, and transgender (LGBT) and queer people, his remarkable phrase is a suitable note on which to end the discussion of spirituality and promiscuity inspired by your case description.

To Eyal

The question is not whether you are Asaf but rather who Asaf is for you so that you took up (verbal) arms against him. Was he your father or other representative of your family, who suddenly came to be a hateful and individuality-swallowing collective force: "Israel"? You say that you "never felt part of their fraternity," which is why I am asking these questions. So there could be a projection of something from your own realm of ghosts onto this client.

I've spent a lot of my career arguing that good clinical practice involves working responsibly with political, social, and cultural material that comes up in analysis. Too often, what we see are the two extremes of (1) a clichéd interpretation in developmental or symbolic terms of such material (often sucking it into the transference–countertransference), or (2) a casual, even impulsive "chat" without any semblance of analytic discipline (as if when the material is political the analyst cannot be expected to be professional).

The really hard thing to do when the matter is political and the tone is disputative, as it was with Asaf, is to facilitate a political discussion. Yet it can be done. Indeed, it has to be done. But none (or very few) of us have had any training as to how to do it. I've found it valuable to break things up into stages so that political discussion within analysis is, so to speak, semistructured.

First, find out the *history* of the piece of material in question. When did Asaf start to feel he wants to return? Was it only when Gaza happened, or earlier? Has there been pressure from home for him to return? Second, working in dialogue, assess the *intensity* attached to the material. How passionate is he about this idea? Is it something he seeks to review, or is it a done deed? Is there a feeling of "ought" around for Asaf, a sense of obligation that may well take him to war but isn't an intense conviction? Third, how *central* to Asaf's sense of self is the wish to return to Israel? The obvious answer may be "absolutely central," but I am not sure—your countertransference wasn't all your stuff, you may have been picking up a strand in Asaf that didn't want to go because he had other things going on in the United States. Finally, after these steps, it might be possible to address any *discrepancy* of viewpoint or values between analyst and client. This is where some "political self-disclosure" may be apposite—based on the work the analyst has done on their political story—and on their political ghosts.

I reprise your use of "ghosts" because we are all in the grip of what I call "political memories," and these are often very early ones. I ask people to tell of their first political memories, the first time they became aware of haves and have-nots, insiders and outsiders, leaders and led, rich and poor. Of war, flight, and famine. Of "abroad." It's amazing how early people's conscious memories of this kind can be. Sure, it is directive, but it is very interesting to elicit such memories from clients. When they arise in the analyst, she or he has the usual disclosure judgment call to make.

There are obvious pitfalls to this approach. The risk of the analyst foisting their views on the client cannot be entirely dismissed. And, if it goes wrong, you do usually lose the client. But if we want to work with "the whole person," and if we want to present as "new objects" to the client, what else are we to do (see Samuels [2006] for a full discussion of these ideas)?

I want to end this letter to you with something that challenges what I sense to be your overall take on political violence and war. I'm doing this because I know I agree with you about what you write about Gaza and what you say to Asaf about the Palestinians. But maybe we both, you and I, have gotten too pacifistic in our thinking. We need to be, given the bellicosity of the three countries we adhere to: Britain, the United States, Israel. Even so, psychoanalytic exploration mustn't run from unpalatable things. Aggressive conflict is an idea that must be addressed by analysts and therapists as much as by political thinkers and politicians. It is very hard to think about aggressive conflict because the topic is so frightening.

Psychoanalysis has worked the aggressive field since its beginnings. One of the main psychoanalytic contributions has been to bring out the hidden relational virtues of aggression. Aggression can lead to getting in touch with the Other, and hence aggression is a mode of relating—a rather useful kind of relating because there is space made for self-interest and self-assertion alongside concern for the Other.

I would like to widen things a bit here. The idea that aggression has its personal uses is echoed by the argument that many liberals and progressives have seriously undervalued aggression in the pursuit of social justice. For example, study of South African politics suggests that without the forceful military contributions of *Umkhonto we Sizwe* ("Spear of the Nation," the military wing of the African National Congress), the South African Communist Party, and the role of mainly Black Cuban troops in Angola, we'd not have seen the new South Africa—no

Nelson Mandela, no Truth and Reconciliation Commission, no books on restorative justice. And, to complicate it even more, all of these developments that were achieved in part by an aggressive response to an undeniably oppressive and aggressive regime were financed and supported by the universally abused Soviet Union. Much the same role for aggression was apparent during the establishment of the State of Israel—and, pertinently, can be argued to be the case with respect of the struggles of the various Palestinian organizations for statehood.

From the point of view of moral philosophy, there is a critical *telos* for aggression. How can you develop concern for an Other if there is no reason to do so? Aggression is required to be present for concern (and the depressive position) to flower. Hence, we lose a lot if we undervalue aggression.

From the point of view of metapsychology, aggression is part of ego consciousness—the way we become conscious in part by breaking wholes into parts. The very etymology of "analysis" is aggressive: Wholes are broken down into parts. And, alongside Klein's (1952) work on oral aggression and sadism, the Israeli Jungian analyst Erich Neumann (1954) wrote that symbols of consciousness itself involved biting and the teeth.

To Avgi

Your case so moved and confused me that I read your text to a group of colleagues who had come to lunch, including a fair range of psychoanalytical orientations and some having worked in psychiatric institutions. One of us was a White American.

The overall response was a compassionate group "Aaaaah," responding to the sweetness at the heart of DeShawn's predicament. There, too, was anger and even contempt for the psychiatric staff who, seemingly willfully, ignored what would here in Britain be regarded as best practice when confronted with a transgendered child—which would certainly not be to "try to make a man of him." We all felt that, aside from the racialized issues to which you refer (and of which more later), there was something to think about in terms of psychodynamic work in inpatient psychiatric settings. The role of the psychodynamic worker, it was felt, is to inform and educate others. We imagined a group discussion involving staff and DeShawn's family convened by yourself.

With that in mind, we found it unsettling that you refer to DeShawn as having a "constitutionally" weak ego. We wondered what this might mean. Chicken and egg, we thought. Suffering such massive rejection of himself at a core identity level was per se an iatrogenic maddening experience, wasn't it? We were thinking R. D. Laing (1960) and radical psychiatry. Anyway, there was a general view that, diagnostically, the boy's ego strength might better be regarded as an unknown factor.

None of us had heard the name DeShawn before, so we Googled it: "Who is like God." We felt that your choice of his name for the piece might have been significant. Those among us with experience of working with religious clients with African heritages felt that the religious dimension might have been important—but of course this was speculative and, I dare say, prejudiced, but we wondered if there was religious content in DeShawn's hallucinations.

Your case narrative is like a detective story, Avgi. First the "problem" seems to be trans- and homophobia. Then it's the sense of racial betrayal and out-of-order behavior. Finally, and this was exquisite clinical work, you created a situation wherein the sex-race blend could be explored on his own in the presence of another by the person to whom it mattered the most: DeShawn.

When I was lecturing in Japan, I learned more about silence on the part of the therapist than the analytical "waiting" to see what will fill the space (which is anything but a genuine openness—more a management of impatience on the part of the clinician). I recognized in your description of your silence the truest form of acceptance of the Other. I envied (admired) you such an experience.

I wonder if you'd agree with the following formulations. DeShawn discovered within himself the need to reject his assigned sex. This was a feeling he knew about and owned. But the rejection of his race was not in fact something that he had discovered within himself. This was a problem for other people. Moreover, in your countertransference fantasy image of DeShawn as a drag entertainer, you can see a route ahead for him in terms of gendered behavior—tough, perhaps, but doable. But race is not a "problem" that excited mental health professionals can "fix" as easily as variant gender. So I am wondering about the symmetry of sex and race here or, perhaps a better way to put it, if they are quite the same from an ontological point of view.

I want to end with a discussion of "unconscious gender certainty" (Samuels, 2001, pp. 38–45) as this played out in DeShawn. Via this formulation, I was attempting to see what might lie behind the consciously experienced gender confusions with which clinicians are generally familiar, and not just in work with transgendered people but with everyone. We all know that behind any tycoon, so capable and dynamic, such a marvelous self-starter, lies a feminine identification so threatening that it has to be removed via overcompensation. For these profound feelings of gender confusion to exist, couldn't there also be an equally profound feeling of gender certainty in operation at some level, a certainty based primarily on internalization from the culture? You cannot know the details of your confusion without having a subliminal inkling of the certitude against which you are measuring it. We could even say: no unconscious gender certainty, no conscious gender confusion. So, to the extent that gender confusion is usually taken as a mental health problem or neurotic conflict, we are making a colossal mistake and even playing a destructive con trick on those supposedly suffering from it. The problem in fact is their gender certainty, carried, in this case narrative, by the staff member Paul. The clinical and the organizational problems are the same problem: to explicate the personal and cultural fetters of unconscious gender certainty.

To Olga

Many of us from refugee backgrounds will have experienced being a "project." Jewish people have long understood that their role is to provide their parents with *nachus*, meaning a sense of a job well done, justifiable pride, and, on the shadow level, competitive success over other parents. These demands constitute precisely the kinds of "impingement" that Winnicott (1965) saw as fundamental to the formation of the false self. And, whatever the intellectual standing of the term, Winnicott believed that there was a "true self" that could be discovered and that "being" as opposed to "doing" was inherent to a true self state.

As a Jungian analyst, I can report that Jungian theory has worked these areas in a slightly different way. Instead of seeing the false self as what covers over a sense of emptiness, we tend to talk about "defenses of the self" (Fordham, 1974), which mask often intense internal activity that often appears in dreams. Lucy's baby dream is a lovely example, and I appreciated that you did not thrust the material into a literal, developmental template, for babies in dreams are often not real babies at all but symbols of rebirth, regeneration, renaissance in an adult.

Another Jungian concept that might be relevant here is that of "individuation," the lifelong process by which persons become who-ever they were "intended" to be. Individuation is as often marked by interruption and distortion as by continuity and truth, and major disruptions can produce negative results. At the same time, contemporary trauma theory has introduced a range of concepts such as posttraumatic growth and adversity-activated development (Papadopoulos, 2007), which, as the language indicates, see immigration as a psychological as well as a material opportunity.

To return to the experience of immigrants, I think it is pretty much accepted that the psychosocial consequences of immigration, undertaken for whatever reason, are intergenerational. Hence, all of your clients are living the unlived psychological lives of their parents and family. Here, too, is the kind of impingement that is false-self friendly. Important aspects of the experience of older generations will crop up in the experience, and hence in the clinical material, of the younger folk.

Papadopoulos (2002), a Jungian analyst, introduced the idea of "nostalgic disorientation" to refer to the uniqueness of an immigrant experience. "The loss is not only about a concrete object or condition but it encapsulates the totality of all the dimensions of home" (p. 15). He explains the classical Greek origins of the term *nostalgia*: *Nostos* means "returning home" and *algos* is ache and pain. Nostalgia, according to Papadopoulos, often means *wanting* to go home. But then Papadopoulos makes a very important point. He says that the desire to go home is not to be taken only (or even at all) in its concrete sense. It also refers to reintegration of the experience of home, but at another level of psychological complexity. Hence, nostalgia is not the regressive and dreamy state that we often take it to be but rather an active pursuit of psychological regeneration. Clinically, Papadopoulos points to the importance of stories, and individuals suffering nostalgic disorientation will need their stories (pp. 14–16).

My question to you is: Did these clients hear enough stories in their early lives and afterwards, and, if they didn't, what can an analyst do about it? Does the analyst have to stay in the world of being? Can she not enter the world of doing, actively helping clients recollect their stories? Is good technique, in which the analyst's desire for the clients' stories would be regarded as in error, really appropriate in such cases?

It goes without saying, I imagine, that the background to these clinical snapshots is a society in which to achieve and compete is all. Unproductive desire, to use your felicitous term, is hardly to be found and certainly not approved of. That is the world of the market. In one sense, it is helpful to newcomers to America because doing well can lead to highly sought-after social mobility. But in many other ways, this is a psychological nightmare for the people involved because of the disavowal of the need to play. On the other hand—and maybe this is something reserved for the upper classes with centuries of safe habitation in one place under their belts—some people see that what looks so real, so adult, so terribly, terribly important is nothing more than a set of childish games.

To Glenys

I'm going to focus on your discovery during the writing of your piece that you had elected to be "color-blind." My interest is in how this client contributed to your "therapy." But first I want to say something about the impact of two rather different "racialized" societies (South Africa and the United States) on this reader, and maybe this is a point of more general interest concerning "reading" in our decidedly international profession of psychoanalysis. You see, I felt that there was no way I could understand the intricacies of race and ethnicity being taken for granted in the clinical discourse. A

Spanish woman in Britain is not usually seen as of a different race, for example. I think that there is an unpleasant paradox here for those of us with an internationalist outlook. Working the fields of cultural and ethnic diversity is a phenomenally local business. This makes dialogue, which is necessary to fight global racial prejudice, very difficult. Hence the ethnic hierarchy organized, as it is, around "Whiteness" remains less challenged than otherwise.

The whole question of the healing role of the client for the analyst is still very difficult to be clear about. Sure, the work in and of itself helps us, whether to fulfill our destiny as the child who wanted to cure the parents or to help us make reparation for excessive aggressivity or to do God's work (or whatever your bag might be). But what about the specific client, such as Martha, who comes along at the right moment? Many clinicians have had such an experience, or more than one. It is a gentle form of synchronicity wherein no rational explanation is likely to be convincing. This is about the meaning of having a particular client, not a causal explanation of how the client gets to you. I've heard it said that we get the clients we deserve, but maybe in addition we get the clients we need.

Naturally, what comes up then are the full range of questions with regard to disclosure. I think the discussions about disclosure (e.g., Davies, 1998; Renik, 1995) generate much more heat than light and the consequences of going one way or the other are greatly exaggerated. I'm not saying it doesn't matter at all, but just thinking out loud that the outcome of such discussions might not matter as much as we believe it does. I guess I am wondering if you felt you had better not acknowledge to Martha what had happened within you.

I am interested in how ethnicized culture gets transmitted over the generations. Improving our understanding might make resignification, if not easy, then easier. I am recalling Jung's (1937) case of a European client who had dreams with Tantric imagery in them, and it turned out she had been raised in Java by an *ayah* (this usually means a nanny, but which Jung took to mean a wet-nurse). Jung exclaimed that the client "had sucked in the local demonology with the *ayah*'s milk" (p. 513). Now, on the scientific or literal level, this is mad. But we lack a posh language to talk about the ways place and culture constitute a matrix from which we evolve. One by-product of this lack is that we are utterly unable to theorize ways subjugated peoples influence the majority culture that has conquered them. In the South Africa of Nellie and Margaret, the "Whites" were (and still are) culturally penetrated by the peoples they had subjugated, regarded as inferior and proposed for separate development. In a sense, this is exactly what happened in your family's séances and use of astrology. And similar kinds of reverse conquests have been written about in terms of Australia with its Aboriginal people—maybe also in the United States. Of course, this may seem far from what psychoanalysis usually deals with. But I don't think it is more far-fetched than the introduction of many concepts from other disciplines.

To conclude, I want to say something about your idea of the "complete Oedipus complex." You make the point that this is culturally nuanced and inflected (and, I would add, changes over time as well). That's what makes it all the more interesting that, from your present vantage point: You don't give as much weight to the "fragile mothers" piece and give more weight to the color blindness. Of course, it is all mixed in together—but it is important that contemporary analysts who want to say something causal don't feel they are restricted to events and happenings in the dim and distant past. Development continues for the whole of life.

Tailing Off

It's very hard to conclude these letters to you with a general comment or statement. You are all so very different. But I would like to reprise some of the things that did concern me. For example, why was there relatively little variation in analytical technique? Or not very much concentration on your power over the client? I am hoping that my remarks on the lack of theorizing about political selfhood in psychoanalytic vein made sense as well as my interest in making work where the political in all its senses moves center stage seem quite boring and conventional.

The note on which I want to go out concerns the analyst as a citizen and the act of psychoanalytic writing as a civic act, with congruent political overtones. I think that the conditions of production and consumption of clinical writing are different from those of clinical work per se. There is a collective aspect in the writing that I see as particularly valuable generally—something accentuated by the political self-awareness of you all as writers.

Thank you for the chance to write to you all.

References

Adelman, A. (1995). Traumatic memory and the intergenerational transmission of Holocaust narratives. *Psychoanalytic Study of the Child*, *50*, 343–367.

Agamben, G. (2005). *State of exception*. (K. Attel, Trans.). Chicago: University of Chicago Press.

Althusser, L. (1971). *Lenin and philosophy*. New York: Monthly Review Press.

Althusser, L. (2001). Ideology and state apparatus. In S. Žižek (Ed.), *Mapping ideologies* (pp. 100–141). NY: Verso. (Original work published 1969)

Altman, N. (2000). Black and White thinking: A psychoanalyst reconsiders race. *Psychoanalytic Dialogues*, *10*, 589–605.

Altman, N. (2004). History repeats itself in transference and countertransference. *Psychoanalytic Dialogues*, *14*, 807–816.

Altman, N. (2006). Whiteness. *Psychoanalytic Quarterly*, *75*, 45–72.

Altman, N. (2009) *The analyst in the inner city: Race, class, and culture through a psychoanalytic lens*. New York and London: Routledge.

Bakhtin, M.M. (1984). *Problems of Dostoevsky's poetics* (p. 287). C. Emerson (Ed. and Trans.). Minneapolis: University of Minnesota Press.

Benjamin, J. (1988). *The bonds of love*. New York: Pantheon.

Benjamin, J. (1994). The omnipotent mother: A psychoanalytic study of fantasy. In D. Bassin, M. Honey, & M. Kaplan (Eds.), *Representations of motherhood* (pp. 129–146). New Haven, CT: Yale University Press.

Benjamin, J. (1995). *Like subjects, love objects*. New Haven, CT: Yale University Press.

Benjamin, J. (1998). *The shadow of the other*. New York: Routledge.

Benjamin, J. (2004). Beyond doer and done to. *Psychoanalytic Quarterly*, 73, 5–46.

Benjamin, J. (2006). Two-way streets: Recognition and difference and the intersubjective third. *Differences: A Journal of Feminist Cultural Studies*, *17*(1), 116–146.

Best, A. (2000). *Prom night: Youth, schools and popular culture*. New York: Routledge.

Bhabha, H. (1994). *The location of culture*. London: Routledge.

Brill, S., & Pepper, R. (2008). *The transgender child: A handbook for families and professionals*. Berkeley, CA: Cleis Press, Inc.

Bromberg, P. (1998). *Standing in the spaces: Essays on clinical process, trauma and dissociation*. Hillsdale, NJ: Analytic Press.

Broyard, B. (2007). *One drop*. New York: Little, Brown and Co.

Bushra, A. (2009). The strangeness of passing: Commentary on paper by Christopher Bonowitz. *Psychoanalytic Dialogues*, *19*, 442–449.

Butler, J. (1990). *Gender trouble: Feminism and the subversion of identity*. New York and London: Routledge.

Butler, J. (1993). *Bodies that matter: On the discursive limits of sex*. New York: Routledge.

Butler, J. (1995). Melancholy gender—Refused identification. *Psychoanalytic Dialogues*, *5*, 165–180.

Butler, J. (1997). *The psychic life of power: Theories in subjection*. Stanford, CA: Stanford University Press.

Butler, J. (2000/1990). *Gender trouble*. New York: Routledge.

Butler, J (2004). Imitation and gender insurbordination. In S. Salin (Ed.), *The Judith Butler reader* (pp. 119–137). Cornwall, UK: Blackwell Publishing.

Caldwell, C., & Keshavan, M. S. (1991). Schizophrenia with secondary trans-sexualism. *Canadian Journal of Psychiatry*, *36*, 300–301.

Carr, E. H. (1964). *What is history?* Harmondsworth, UK: Penguin.

Chaplin, J. (2005). The Bridge Project: Radical psychotherapy for the 21st century. In N. Totton (Ed.), *The politics of psychotherapy*. New York: Open University Press.

Chodorow, N. (1978). T*he reproduction of mothering: Psychoanalysis and the sociology of gender*. Berkeley: University of California Press.

Coates, S. W., & Moore, M. S. (1998). The complexity of early trauma: Representation and transformation. In D. DiCeglie (Ed.), *A stranger in my own body: Atypical gender identity development and mental health* (pp. 39–62). London: Karnac Books.

Cole, J. B., & Guy-Sheftal, B. (2003). *Gender talk: The struggle for women's equality in African American communities*. New York: Ballantine.

Collins, P. H. (2005). *Black sexual politics: African Americans, gender and the new racism*. New York: Routledge.

Corbett, K. (1996). Homosexual boyhood: Notes on girlyboys. *Gender and Psychoanalysis*, *1*, 429–461.

Corbett, K. (1997). Speaking queer: A reply to Richard C. Friedman. *Gender and Psychoanalysis*, *2*, 495–514.

Corbett, K. (2009). *Boyhoods*. New Haven, CT: Yale University Press.

Curtis, A. (Writer/Director). (2004). *The power of nightmares: The rise of the politics of fear* [Motion picture]. United Kingdom: BBC.

Cushman, P. (1995). *Constructing the self, constructing America: A cultural history of psychotherapy*. Reading, MA: Addison-Wesley.

Davies, J. M. (1998). Between the disclosure and foreclosure of erotic transference-countertransference. *Psychoanalytic Dialogues, 8,* 747–766.

De Marneffe, D. (2004). *Maternal desire: On children, love, and the inner life*. New York: Little, Brown and Co.

DiCeglie, D. (1998a). Management and therapeutic aims in working with children and adolescents with gender identity disorder, and their families. In D. DiCeglie (Ed.), *A stranger in my own body: Atypical gender identity development and mental health* (pp. 185–197). London: Karnac Books.

DiCeglie, D. (1998b). Reflections on the nature of the "atypical gender identity organization." In D. DiCeglie (Ed.), *A stranger in my own body: Atypical gender identity development and mental health* (pp. 9–25). London: Karnac Books.

DiCeglie, D. (1998c). "William": Working with the family about unresolved mourning and secrecy. In D. DiCeglie (Ed.), *A stranger in my own body: Atypical gender identity development and mental health* (pp. 249–254). London: Karnac Books.

Dimen, M. (1991). Deconstructing difference: Gender, splitting and transitional space. *Psychoanalytic Dialogues, 1,* 335–352.

Dimen, M. (1995). Introduction: Symposium on sexuality/sexualities. *Psychoanalytic Dialogues, 5*(2), 157–164.

Dimen, M. (2003). *Sexuality, intimacy, power*. Hillsdale, NJ: The Analytic Press.

Dimen, M. (2007). Ma vie en rose: A meditation. In M. Suchet, A. Harris, & L. Aron (Eds.), *Relational psychoanalysis, vol. III: New voices* (pp. 53–60). Mahwah, NJ: Analytic Press.

Dimen, M. (2011), Lapsus linguae, or a slip of the tongue? A sexual violation in an analytic treatment and its personal and theoretical aftermath. *Contemporary Psychoanalysis, 47*(1), 35–79.

Dimen, M. & Goldner, V. (2005), Gender and sexuality. In E.S. Person, A.M. Cooper, and G.O. Gabbard (Eds.), *The American psychiatric publishing textbook of psychoanalysis* (pp. 93–116). Washington, DC: American Psychiatric Publishing, Inc.

Eichenbaum, L., & Orbach, S. (1982). *Understanding women*. New York: Basic Books.

Eng, D. L., & Han, S. (2000). A dialogue on racial melancholia. *Psychoanalytic Dialogues, 10,* 677–700.

Fanon, F. (1967). *Black skin, White masks*. New York: Grove.

Ferguson, R. A. (2004). *Aberrations in black: Toward a queer of color critique*. Minneapolis: University of Minnesota Press.

Ferguson, R. A. (2005). Race-ing homonormativity: Citizenship, sociology, and gay identity. In E. P. Johnson & M. G. Henderson (Eds.), *Black queer studies: An anthology* (pp. 52–67). Durham, NC: Duke University Press.

Fonagy, P., & Target, M. (1996). Playing with reality: I. Theory of mind and the normal development of psychic reality. *International Journal of Psychoanalysis*, 77, 217–233.

Fordham, M. (1974). *The self and autism*. London: Heinemann.

Foucault, M. (1977). *Discipline and punish*. New York: Pantheon.

Foucault, M. (1988–90) *History of sexuality* (Vols. 1–3). (R. Hurley, Trans.). New York: Vintage Books. (Original work published 1976)

Foucault, M. (2005). *The hermeneutics of the subject: Lectures at the College de France, 1981–1982*. New York: Picador.

Fowler, J. C. (1999). Some reflections on self-mutilations. *Psychoanalytic Review*, 86, 719–729.

Friedan, B. (1963). *The feminine mystique*. New York: Simon & Shuster.

Freud, A., & Burlingham, D. (1943). *War and children*. New York: Medical War Books.

Freud, S. (1914). On narcissism. In J. Strachey (Ed. & Trans.), *The standard edition of the complete psychological works of Sigmund Freud* (Vol. 14, pp. 67–102). London: Hogarth Press.

Freud, S. (1961). *Civilization and its discontents*. (J. Strachey, Trans.). New York: Norton. (Original work published 1930)

Freund-Chertok, H. (2010). *Radical body art: A philosophical analysis*. Unpublished PhD thesis, The Cohn Institute for the History and Philosophy of Science and Ideas, Tel Aviv University.

Gerson, S. (2009). When the third is dead: Memory, mourning, and witnessing in the after .... *International Journal of Psychoanalysis*, 90, 1341–1357.

Goldner, V. (1991). Toward a critical relational theory of gender. *Psychoanalytic Dialogues*, 1, 249–272.

Goldner, V. (2006, April). *Trans: A gender theorist's (wet) dream ... and nightmare*. Paper presented at the Division 39 Meeting of the American Psychological Association, Philadelphia, PA.

Gonzalez, F. (2009, May). *Negative Oedipus redux: Transfigurations of a field; Part one: Ex nihilo—Precocity and negation*. Paper presented to the Psychoanalytic Institute of Northern California, San Francisco.

Goss, R. (2004). Proleptic sexual love: God's promiscuity reflected in Christian polyamory. *Theology and Sexuality*, 11(1), 52–63.

Greenberg, J. & Mitchell, S. A. (1983), *Object relations in psychoanalytic theory*. Cambridge, MA: Harvard University Press.

Greer, G. (1970). *The female eunuch*. New York: Pantheon.

Guralnik, O. (2007, April). Standing in the spaces between interpellation and dissociation. Paper presented at the Division 39 Meeting of the American Psychological Association, Toronto, ON.

Guralnik, O. & Simeon, D. (2001). Self-mutilation: Psychodynamic treatment. In D. Simeon & E. Hollander (Eds.), *Self-injurious behaviors: Assessment and treatment* (pp. 175–198). New York: American Psychological Association.

Guralnik, O. & Simeon, D. (2010). Depersonalization: Standing in the spaces between recognition and interpellation. *Psychoanalytic Dialogues*, *20*, 400–416.

Harlem, A. (2009) Thinking through others: Cultural psychology and the psychoanalytic treatment of immigrants. *Psychoanalysis, Culture, and Society*, *14*, 273–288.

Harris, A. (2005). Gender in linear and nonlinear history. *Journal of the American Psychoanalytic Association*, *53*, 1079–1095.

Harris, A. (2007a). The house of difference: Enactment, a play in three scenes. In M. Suchet, A. Harris, & L. Aron (Eds.), *Relational psychoanalysis, vol. 3: New voices* (pp. 81–96). Mahwah, NJ: Analytic Press.

Harris, A. (2007b). Discussion of "Unraveling Whiteness." *Psychoanalytic Dialogues*, *17*, 887–894.

Harris, A. (2008). *Gender as soft assembly*. New York: Routledge.

Hartman, S. (2010), Ruined by pleasure: Commentary on Steven Botticelli and Jeffrey R. Guss. *Studies in Gender and Sexuality*, 11(3), 141–145.

Heymann S. J., Earle, A., and Hayes, J. (2007). *The work, family, and equity index: How does the United States measure up?* Retrieved January 8, 2011, from McGill University, Institute for Health and Social Policy Web site: http://www.mcgill.ca/files/ihsp/WFE12007FINAL.pdf

hooks, b. (1995). *Killing rage: Ending racism*. New York: Owl.

hooks, b. (2004). *We real cool: Black men and masculinity*. New York: Routledge.

Hopkins, L. B. (2000). Masud Khan's application of Winnicott's "play" techniques to analytic consultation and treatment of adults. *Contemporary Psychoanalysis*, *36*, 639–663.

Horney, K. (1967). *Feminine psychology*. New York: Norton.

Hyde, A. (2007). *Bodies of law*. Princeton, NJ: Princeton University Press.

Juhasz, S. (2003). *A desire for women: Relational psychoanalysis, writing, and relationships between women*. New Brunswick, NJ: Rutgers University Press.

Jung, C. G. (1937). The role of the unconscious. In *Civilization in transition: Collected works, vol. 10*. Princeton, NJ: Princeton University Press.

Kestenberg, J. S. (1980). Psychoanalyses of children of survivors from the Holocaust: Case presentations and assessment. *Journal of the American Psychoanalytic Association*, *28*, 775–804.

Klein, M. (1952). Some theoretical conclusions regarding the emotional life of the infant. In J. Rivière, (Ed.), *Developments in psychoanalysis* (pp. 61–71). London: Hogarth.

Klein, M. (1964). Love, guilt and reparation. In M. Klein & J. Rivière (Eds.), *Love, hate & reparation*. NY: Norton.

Klueger, R. (2004). *Simple justice: The history of* Brown v. Board of Education *and Black America's struggle for equality*. New York: Vintage Books Edition.

Knafo, D. (2009). Castration and Medusa: Orlan's art on the cutting edge. *Studies in Gender and Sexuality*, *10*, 142–158.

Kristeva, J. (1998). The subject in process, In P. French & J.-F. Lack (Eds.), *The Tel Quel reader* (pp. 133–178). New York: Routledge.

Laing, R.D. (1960). *The divided self*. Harmondsworth: Penguin.

Lasch, C. (1979). *The culture of narcissism: American life in an age of diminishing expectations*. New York: Warner Books.

Laufer, E. M. (1991). Body image, sexuality and the psychotic core. *International Journal of Psychoanalysis, 72*, 63–71.

Layton, L. (2006a). Racial identities, racial enactments, and normative unconscious processes. *Psychoanalytic Quarterly, 75*, 237–270.

Layton, L. (2006b). Attacks on linking: The unconscious pull to dissociate individuals from their social context. In L. Layton, N. C. Hollander, & S. Gutwill (Eds.), *Psychoanalysis, class and politics* (pp. 107–117). London: Routledge.

Lazarre, J. (1991). *Worlds beyond my control*. New York: Dutton.

Leary, K. (2000). Racial enactments in dynamic treatment. *Psychoanalytic Dialogues, 10*, 639–653.

Lev, A. I. (2004). *Transgender emergence: Therapeutic guidelines for working with gender variant people and their families*. New York: Haworth Press.

Levenson, E. (1983). *The ambiguity of change*. New York: Basic Books.

MacKinnon, K. (2005). *Women's lives, men's laws*. Boston: Harvard University Press.

McRuer, M. (2006). *Crip theory: Cultural signs of queerness and disability*. New York: New York University Press.

Mitchell, J. (1974). *Psychoanalysis and feminism*. London: Allen Lane.

Morrison, T. (1992). *Jazz*. New York: Vintage

Neal, M. A. (2006). *New Black man*. New York: Routledge.

Neumann, E. (1954). *The origins and history of consciousness*. London: Routledge/ Kegan Paul.

Ogden, T. H. (1995). Analyzing forms of aliveness and deadness of the transference-countertransference. *International Journal of Psychoanalysis, 76*, 695–709.

Ooi, K. G. (2004). *Southeast Asia: A historical encyclopedia, from Angkor Wat to East Timor*. Santa Barbara, CA: ABC-CLIO.

Orbach, S. (1978). *Fat is a feminist issue*. London: Paddington Press.

Orbach, S. (2009). *BODIES*. London: Profile Books.

Papadopoulos, R. (2002). Refugees, home and trauma. In *Therapeutic care for refugees: No place like home* (pp. 9–40). London: Karnac.

Papadopoulos, R. (2007). Refugees, trauma and adversity-activated development. *European Journal of Psychotherapy and Counseling, 9*(3), 301–312.

Pascoe, C. J. (2007). *Dude, you are a fag*. Berkeley: University of California Press.

Perry, P. (2002). *Shades of White: White kids and racial identities in high school*. Durham, NC: Duke University Press.

Pitt, L. (2004). Crazy sometimes. In B. Singley (Ed.), *When race becomes real*. New York: Lawrence Hill.

Reich, W. (1970). *The mass psychology of fascism*. New York: Farrar, Straus & Giroux.

Reich, W. (1972). *Sex-pol essays, 1929–34*. New York: Vintage.

Reich, W. (1974). *The sexual revolution*. New York: Macmillan.

Renik, O. (1995). The ideal of the anonymous analyst and the problem of self-disclosure. *Psychoanalytic Quarterly, 64*, 466–495.

Rivera, M. (1989). Linking the psychological and the social: Feminism, post-structuralism and multiple personality. *Dissociation, 2*, 24–30.

Roth, P. (2001). *The dying animal.* London: Vintage, 2006.

Samuels, A. (1985). *Jung and the post-Jungians.* London: Routledge/Kegan Paul.

Samuels, A. (1999). *Queer therapy: A new standard of excellence for clinical practice in the psychotherapy field.* Unpublished manuscript.

Samuels, A. (2001). *Politics on the couch: Citizenship and the internal life.* London: Karnac.

Samuels, A. (2006). Working directly with political, social and cultural material in the therapy session. In L. Layton, N. C. Hollander, & S. Gutwill (Eds.), *Psychoanalysis, class and politics: Encounters in the clinical setting* (pp. 11–28). London: Routledge.

Samuels, A. (2010). Promiscuities: Politics, imagination, spirituality and hypocrisy. In M. Barker & D. Landridge (Eds.), *Understanding non-monogamies* (pp. 212–224). London: Routledge.

Sheehy, M. (2004, February). Attachment anxiety. *Child,* pp. 65ff.

Siomopoulos, V. (1974). Transsexualism: Disorder of gender identity, thought disorder or both? *Journal of the American Academy of Psychoanalysis, 2*, 201–213.

Slavin, J. H., Oxenhandler, N., Seligman, S., Stein, R. and Davies, J. M. (2004). Dialogues on sexuality in development and treatment. *Studies in Gender and Sexuality, 5*(4), 371–418.

Stoller, R. J. (1966). The mother's contribution to infantile transvestitic behavior. *International Journal of Psychoanalysis, 47*, 384–395.

Stoller, R. J. (1968). *Sex and gender: On the development of masculinity and femininity.* New York: Science House.

Stoller, R. J. (1970). Psychotherapy of extremely feminine boys. *International Journal of Psychiatry, 9*, 278–281.

Stoller, R. J. (1975). Primary femininity. *Journal of the American Psychoanalytic Association, 24*(Suppl.), 59–78.

Straker, G. (2004). Race for cover: Castrated Whiteness, perverse consequences. *Psychoanalytic Dialogues, 14*, 405–422.

Straker, G. (2006). The anti-analytic third. *Psychoanalytic Review, 93*, 729–753.

Straker, G. (2007). The crisis in the subjectivity of the analyst: The trauma of morality. *Psychoanalytic Dialogues, 17*, 153–164.

Strenger, C. (2004). *The designed self: Psychoanalysis and contemporary identities.* Hillsdale, NJ: The Analytic Press.

Suchet, M. (2004), A relational encounter with race. *Psychoanalytic Dialogues, 14*, 423–438.

Suchet, M. (2007). Unraveling Whiteness. *Psychoanalytic Dialogues, 17*, 867–886.

Tacey, D. (2000). *The uses of enchantment.* Sydney: HarperCollins.

The World Bank. (2010). *The World Bank in Nigeria 1998–2007: Nigeria country assistance evaluation*. Retrieved January 8, 2011, from http://siteresources. worldbank.org/EXTCOUASSEVAL/Resources/nigeria_cae.pdf

Walton, G. (2005). Bullying and homophobia in Canadian schools: The politics of policies, programs and educational leadership. In J. Sears (Ed.), *Gay, lesbian, and transgender issues in education: Programs, policies and practices* (pp. 89–104). New York: Harrington Park Press.

Warner, J. (2005). *Perfect madness: Motherhood in the age of anxiety*. New York: Riverhead Books.

West, C. (1993). *Race matters*. Boston: Beacon Press.

Wilson, A. (1985). On silence and the Holocaust: A contribution to clinical theory. *Psychoanalytic Inquiry, 5*, 63–84.

Winnicott, D. W. (1965). True and false self. In *The maturational processes and the facilitating environment* (pp. 140–152). London: Hogarth Press.

Zaehner, R. (1957). *Mysticism: Sacred and profane*. Oxford: Oxford University Press.

Author Index

Neumann, E., 172
Nietzsche, F., 70

O

Obama, B., 85–86, 161
Ogden, T.H., 152
Ooi, K.G., 68
Orbach, S., 6, 7
Orlan, 71
Oxenhandler, N., 102

P

Papadopoulos, R., 175–176
Pappenheim, B., 56
Pascoe, C.J., 147
Pepper, R., 144
Perry, P., 147
Pitt, L., 42
Pugachevsky, O., 6, 31–34, 54–56, 93–97, 117, 149–154

R

Reich, W., 7, 108
Renik, O., 177
Rivera, M., 81
Roth, P., 168
Rozmarin, E., 6, 35–40, 49, 58–60, 87–91, 137–142

S

Saketopoulou, A., 6, 143–148
Samuels, A., 6, 7, 163–179

Seligman, S., 102
Sheehy, M., 6, 11–17, 50, 99–105, 108, 118
Simeon, D., 68, 69
Siomopoulos, V., 145
Slavin, J.H., 102
Stein, R., 102
Stelarc, 71
Stoller, R.J., 144
Straker, G., 84, 157
Strenger, C., 70
Suchet, M., 84, 157
Sutherland, D., 79

T

Target, M., 144
Thomas, C., 44

W

Walton, G., 144
Warner, J., 15
West, C., 147
Wilson, A., 96
Winnicott, D.W., 174
Wurman, V., 107

Z

Zaehner, R., 169
Zaphiropoulos, L., 107

Subject Index